About the author

Graham Burton teaches on courses in English for Academic Purposes and General English at the University of Bolzano, and lectures at the University of Trento, both in northern Italy. He has also taught at a number of schools and universities in the UK and in Greece.

Acknowledgements

I would like to thank all the team at HarperCollins, in particular Celia Wigley, and my editors Estelle Jobson and Sarah Curtis for their support and help, and also the project manager Verity Cole. I am also grateful to my wife Anita, and daughter Sofia. Finally, special thanks to Nick Robinson for his invariably wise advice and invaluable support.

Contents

Collins
E A P

Presenting

Deliver presentations
with confidence

Graham Burton

Skills Series

Collins

HarperCollins Publishers
77-85 Fulham Palace Road
Hammersmith
London W6 8JB

First edition 2013

Reprint 10 9 8 7 6 5 4 3 2 1 0

© HarperCollins Publishers 2013

ISBN 978-0-00-750713-9

Collins® is a registered trademark of HarperCollins Publishers Limited

www.collinselt.com

A catalogue record for this book is available from the British Library

Typeset in India by Aptara

Printed in China by South China Printing Co.

◐ You can trust Collins COBUILD

The 4.5-billion-word Collins Corpus is the world's largest database of the English language. It is updated every month and has been at the heart of Collins COBUILD publishing for over 20 years. All definitions provided in the glossary boxes in this book have been taken from the Collins COBUILD Advanced Dictionary.

The Publisher and author wish to thank the following rights holders for the use of copyright material:

Extract from Take it Personally by Anita Roddick reprinted by permission of HarperCollins Publishers Ltd (2001) Anita Roddick

Extract from The Age of Consent by George Monbiot (2010) reprinted by permission of HarperCollins Publishers Ltd

Extract from Click: What we do online and why it matters by Bill Tancer (2008) reprinted by permission of HarperCollins Publishers Ltd and Hyperion

Lecture "Happiness: has social science got a clue?" by Richard Layard, the Lionel Robbins Memorial Lectures, March 2003 reproduced by permission of Richard Layard

Clip Art used by permission of Microsoft

Images from Shutterstock except for Clip Art on page 112.

If any copyright holders have been omitted, please contact the Publisher who will make the necessary arrangements at the first opportunity.

Contents

POWERED BY COBUILD

Introduction

Collins Academic Skills Series: Presenting will give you the skills you need to give a successful presentation in an academic context.

Designed to be used on a self-study basis to support English for Academic Purposes or study skills courses, it is intended for students on pre-sessional or Foundation courses as well as for first year undergraduate students.

The book has twelve chapters covering all the areas needed to give a successful presentation. You will learn how to:

- speak and present in seminars and tutorials
- plan, structure and rehearse your presentation
- speak from notes and use your voice effectively
- use body language and eye contact
- engage your audience
- create and use visual aids, including PowerPoint presentations
- deal with nerves and overcome problems
- create and give poster presentations

At the back of the book there are:

- useful reference materials to help you give successful presentations, including photocopiable forms that you can use again and again
- a glossary of key terms
- an audioscript
- a comprehensive answer key

Chapter structure

Each chapter includes:

- Aims – These set out the skills covered in the chapter.
- A self-evaluation quiz – By doing this you are able identify what you already know on the subject of the chapter and what you need to learn.
- Information on academic expectations and guidelines on how to develop academic skills – These sections will help you understand university practices and expectations so you know what is required.
- Practical exercises – These help you to develop the skills to succeed at university. You can check your answers at the back of the book.

- Tips – Key points are highlighted for easy reference and provide useful revision summaries for the busy student.
- Glossary – Difficult words are glossed in boxes next to where the text appears in the chapter. There is also a comprehensive glossary at the back of the book.
- Remember sections – This is a summary of key points for revision and easy reference.

Glossary boxes ⊆ POWERED BY COBUILD

Where we feel that a word or phrase is difficult to understand, we have glossed this word/phrase. All definitions provided in the glossary boxes have been taken from the *COBUILD Advanced Dictionary*. At the end of the book there is a full alphabetical list of the most difficult words from the book for your reference.

Using *Presenting*

You can either work through the chapters from Chapter 1 to Chapter 12 or you can choose the chapters and topics that are most useful to you. The Contents page will help in your selection.

Study tips

- Each chapter will take about two to three hours. Take regular breaks and do not try to study for too long. Thirty to sixty minutes is a sensible study period.
- Regular study is better than occasional intensive study.
- Read the chapter through first to get an overview without doing any exercises. This will help you see what you want to focus on.
- Try the exercises before checking the Answer key. Be an active learner.
- All university departments are different. Use the information in the book as a guide to investigating your own university department.
- Write questions you can ask to find out how your department expects you to give a presentation.
- There is no one correct way of giving a presentation. Use your experience of doing the exercises to learn what works best for you. Adapt the suggestions in this book to suit your learning style and context.
- Learning to present is an on-going process, which means you need to practise the same skills many times. Revise regularly.

Other titles

Also available in the *Collins Academic Skills Series: Research, Writing, Lectures, Numbers,* and *Group Work*.

1 | Presenting at university

Aims
- ✓ understand reasons for giving presentations
- ✓ learn about types of presentation
- ✓ understand common fears about presentations
- ✓ learn about features of a good presentation

Aims

? Quiz
Self-evaluation

Read the statements, then circle the word which is true for you.

1	I understand why universities often ask students to give presentations.	agree | disagree | not sure
2	I know the different types of presentation I might be asked to give.	agree | disagree | not sure
3	I know some common worries students have about giving presentations.	agree | disagree | not sure
4	I understand what makes a good presentation.	agree | disagree | not sure

Tip ✓ The tertiary education institution you go to after high school can be called different names. In the USA, people talk about university, school and college. In the UK, people tend to call it university ('uni') and college. In South Africa, people refer to university ('varsity'), technikon, technical training college, or generally to institutes of further education and training. In Australia it is university or 'uni' and TAFE which is technical and further education.

Tip

Why students are required to give presentations

Glossary

English-medium
If a school or university is English-medium, then English is the language used for teaching there.

At English-medium universities, it is very common for students to be asked to give a presentation. The kind of presentation, and how many you have to give, depends on the university and the subject you are studying.

Many students do not like giving presentations. The idea of giving a presentation in front of a group of people may sound more difficult than writing an essay or an exam. If your first language is not English, then giving a presentation in it will probably seem even more difficult. On top of all this, you probably will not be taught how to give a presentation in your course – you may be expected to work everything out yourself. Even so, once you have completed your first presentation, you will probably feel proud of yourself. Presentations normally get easier, the more of them you do. They also give you the chance to develop useful skills.

There are plenty of reasons why your university might ask you to give a presentation as part of your studies. Presentations help students in these ways.

- Doing presentations helps students develop new skills that may be useful in a future career.

- They prepare students to give presentations at conferences (e.g. if they work as researchers or in sales and marketing).

- They give students useful skills for later job searches; presentations are often part of job interviews.

- They encourage independent research.

- They help students to develop group work skills (e.g. when doing group presentations).

- While some students plagiarize in their written assignments, it is very difficult to cheat while giving a presentation.

- They help students to develop their knowledge of a specific topic.

- They help students to develop self-confidence.

- If students are assessed for their presentations, this gives those students who do not perform as well in exams or other written work a better chance to get a good mark overall.

- By going through a process of researching, preparing and then giving a presentation, students will learn more than by just reading information or attending a lecture.

Types of presentation

You could be asked to give a presentation at different stages of your studies and for different reasons. You might have to give a presentation that is not assessed, meaning you will not receive a mark. Your presentation might, however, contribute significantly to the final score for your course.

Some of the most common types of presentation are:

- seminar and tutorial discussions
- seminar papers
- seminar presentations
- poster presentations

 Exercise 1

Match the different presentation types, 1–4, to the descriptions, a–d.

1 seminar and tutorial discussions	a presenting a topic individually or in a group to your seminar group
2 seminar papers	b producing a visual summary of research you have done and talking about it
3 seminar presentations	c discussing a topic with a teacher and a small number of other students
4 poster presentations	d introducing a topic to your seminar group, often including preparing a written text to give to your teacher

You will look at all these types of presentation in the rest of this book. In Chapter 12, you will learn about poster presentations, which are quite different from other types of presentation.

 Tip ✓ The word 'tutorial' is used in different ways at different universities and in their different departments. For more information on how the word is used, see Chapter 2.

Problems and worries

As you read in the previous section, there are a number of positive aspects of being asked to give a presentation. However, many students see presentations as something to worry about rather than something to benefit from. The following fears are very common:

- feeling nervous or uncomfortable speaking in public,
- worrying that your language skills are not good enough,
- feeling you do not know enough about the topic,
- being concerned that people will ask questions you will not be able to answer,
- not knowing what content to include and how to organize it,
- worrying about working with other students for a group presentation.

Exercise 2

Read the information about the typical worries students have about presentations and complete the gaps with the following phrases.

a do not know enough about the topic

b give presentations in groups

c language skills

d speaking in public

e worry about what to include

1 Most people feel nervous about _____ – even very experienced speakers do. Nerves can actually be helpful, though, as adrenalin (the substance your body produces when you are angry, excited or frightened which makes your heart beat faster), can give you more energy and focus.

2 International students often worry about their _____ . This is understandable. If this is true for you, remember that you probably have an advantage over many native speakers – if you had to do several English language exams to get into university, you may be more used to having your speaking skills assessed.

3 When you first think about the idea of giving a presentation, it is normal to feel you _____ . But once you start preparing your presentation, this worry should disappear, because during your preparation, you will become more knowledgeable about your topic.

4 At the beginning of the process, it is normal to _____ in the presentation and how to organize it. However, with good research and preparation, this will not be a problem.

5 Sometimes students worry if they are asked to _____ . Working with other students can create different challenges, especially if you do not know the other people in the group very well or they are a different nationality to you. By working in a group you will develop useful skills, such as sharing your ideas, listening and acknowledging other people's ideas. You might find that you get support from the other people in your group, unlike when you do an individual presentation.

For more information on preparing and dealing with nerves, see Chapter 10.

The features of a good presentation

You may be asked to give different types of presentation during your studies. The specific course you are studying and the requirements from your university will influence your final presentation. However, there are some important things you should always think about, whatever kind of presentation you need to give.

Exercise 3

Look at the list below. Tick the things you think are important and appropriate for a university presentation. Add three more features you think are important at the end of the list.

- anticipating problems
- using effective body language and eye contact
- using visual aids effectively
- engaging with your audience
- giving as much detail as possible
- being well organized
- making the audience laugh
- planning and rehearsing
- including relevant content
- speaking effectively
- writing a script and reading it carefully
- _____
- _____
- _____

Exercise 4

Think about the three features from Exercise 3 that you should not have selected. Why are these things unimportant and inappropriate for a university presentation?

Exercise 5

Read the explanations and examples below. Complete the gaps by writing one of the features you selected in Exercise 3.

1   having a clear introduction, main part and conclusion, and keeping to the time limit: _____

2   talking about things the audience will be interested in and will not already know: _____

3   speaking from notes instead of from a script and using your voice effectively, with clear pronunciation: _____

4   using your body to make your message clear, and making eye contact with your audience: _____

5   capturing the interest of your audience and getting them involved: _____

6   using tools like PowerPoint, handouts and overhead projectors to support your presentation: _____

7   organizing the time you have to prepare and practise your presentation in advance: _____

8   thinking about and planning ahead for things that might go wrong: _____

By working through this book, you will learn how to improve your skills in all these areas.

Remember

✓   Although presentations are often very difficult, they can teach you many skills and can be useful in your future career.

✓   Be prepared to give different types of presentations during your studies.

✓   Although you may have concerns about presentations, your nerves can actually help your performance on the day. If you prepare for your presentation properly, you should not have serious problems.

✓   Think about the specific features that good presentations have in common.

2 | Seminars and tutorials

Aims ✓ understand the difference between
seminars and tutorials

✓ understand the difference between
seminar presentations and seminar
papers

✓ take part in seminar discussions

✓ give a seminar paper

? Quiz
Self-evaluation

Read the statements, then circle the word which is true for you.

1	I know the difference between seminars and tutorials.	agree | disagree | not sure
2	I understand the difference between seminar presentations and seminar papers.	agree | disagree | not sure
3	I feel confident taking part in seminars: expressing my ideas, getting a chance to speak, getting information, agreeing and disagreeing.	agree | disagree | not sure
4	I know how to give a seminar paper.	agree | disagree | not sure

Seminars and tutorials

Glossary

set
If a book is a set work (or 'set'), it means you are obliged to read it for your studies.

distinction
A distinction between similar things is a difference.

Different universities and even departments within universities use the words 'seminar' and 'tutorial' in different ways. Generally, seminars are meetings with a lecturer and a fairly small group of students. Usually, a seminar has no more than 20 students, but it can be much smaller.

In a seminar, you might:

- discuss the contents of a lecture you attended,

- discuss the set reading for the week,

- do problem-solving exercises,

- present a summary of some reading you have done or some research you are doing.

Sometimes, the lecturer asks a different student to lead a discussion each week or from time to time.

Tutorials, on the other hand, are usually much smaller – perhaps with only two or three students and one lecturer. In tutorials, students can work through a problem or discuss their written work. In a tutorial, you will probably not have to prepare and give a presentation, but you will need to discuss and present your ideas. Not all universities offer tutorials, however.

Some universities and departments use the word 'tutorial' to mean 'seminar'. In this book, however, we will keep the distinction between the two.

Differences between seminar presentations and seminar papers

Glossary

handbook
A handbook is a book that gives you advice and instructions about a particular subject.

Two common phrases you might hear in the context of seminars are 'seminar paper' and 'seminar presentation'. Again, not all universities and departments use these phrases in the same way. To find out how your university uses these terms and to check exactly what you will be expected to do, read your student handbook and the information available about your courses very carefully.

The seminar paper

Glossary

aloud
When you say something, read, or laugh aloud, you speak or laugh so that other people can hear you.

If you are asked to give a seminar paper, you may have to prepare some kind of written paper in advance. Then, in the seminar, you may need to lead a discussion of it, perhaps reading aloud all or part of your paper. If your lecturer gives you a mark, it might be for the written paper only, which they will assess separately. In some universities, every week a different student is asked to lead a seminar, but the student is not formally assessed.

In either case, the most important thing is normally the content of what you say, not how well you say it.

A seminar presentation

Normally, if you are asked to do a seminar presentation, you should give a presentation, but do not need to hand in a paper as well. You will be assessed not just on what you say (the content of the presentation), but on how you present it and on the visual aids you use. You will learn more about seminar presentations working through this book.

As explained, not all universities use these terms in the same way. Sometimes, 'seminar paper' refers to a seminar presentation and sometimes to the presenting part of a seminar paper only. However, in this book, the definitions provided here are used.

Exercise 1

Have you received your student handbook? If so, check to see if the terms 'seminar' and 'tutorial' are used at your university and find out what these words mean. Usually, you can find a student handbook on your university's website. The section for international students is often particularly useful.

Do you know what courses you will be taking? If you have information on any of your courses, read through it to see if students need to give presentations. Will your presentations be assessed or not? How do the requirements for your courses differ from what you have learned here about seminar presentations and papers?

Discussions in seminars and tutorials

In both seminars and tutorials, you benefit from participating in the discussions. On some courses, part of your final assessment might come from your involvement in seminars. But even if you are not assessed, seminar discussions give you a chance to ask for explanations, to check your ideas and to hear other opinions, those of your lecturer and the other students. This participation can be extremely helpful later in your studies, when you write an assignment or do an exam.

Many students find participating in seminars difficult. This can be for several reasons.

Students may feel:

- worried about making mistakes and appearing stupid,

- unable to think or react quickly enough,

- that they have nothing interesting or new to say,

- worried if their performance is being assessed,

- that they do not completely understand the topic being discussed.

Exercise 2

Look again at the problems listed. Are any of these difficulties true for you? Try to write a solution to or reason for the problems.

It is important to always attend your seminars and tutorials and to participate actively. They help you make your own studying more effective. Furthermore, they create the chance for you and your lecturers to get to know each other.

Expressing ideas

In Exercise 2, you considered how important it is, when preparing for a seminar, to think about your own reactions and opinions to what you have read or heard in a lecture. To share your views, use the following useful phrases.

Expressing ideas

I think …
I would say that …
In my view, …
In my opinion, …
It seems to me that …

In academic writing or speaking, it is not common to give very emphatic opinions (e.g. 'I'm certain that …') Instead, it is often common to show that there is a possibility that what you are saying is incorrect, using words like 'could' or 'possibly'. There are many reasons for doing this, but perhaps the most important is that it can be dangerous to appear too confident, because there may be other research that you are not aware of that contradicts what you are saying, or even research in the future that will do this. Avoiding emphatic opinions is sometimes called hedging.

Exercise 3

Read the following sentences. In each sentence, underline the word or words that make the speaker's opinion appear less strong.

1   It seems that most governments in the world aren't interested in stopping climate change.

2   Perhaps we need to think about parenting in a different context.

3   The policy might work better in the developed world.

4   I'd say there are a lot of reasons why the cold war ended.

5   In a sense, both writers are making the same point about modernism.

6   Maybe stable prices are impossible in the economy at the moment.

7   I think, in a way, that looking at human rights as universal isn't always right.

8   I think it's sort of old-fashioned to think of the internet like that.

Exercise 4

Rewrite the sentences below so they are less emphatic. You can use the phrases from Exercise 3.

1   The EU's economic policies aren't working.

2   The people interviewed for the survey don't represent the whole of society.

3   There were other reasons for the conflict.

4   In the future, the email system like it is today won't exist any more.

5   It wasn't a free and fair election.

In seminars, you also often need to be able to discuss reasons. Use the following useful phrases.

> **Explaining reasons**
>
> One reason for ... is ...
> ... happens because ...
> That's (the reason) why ...
> That's because ...
> One explanation (of ...) is ...

Getting a chance to speak and using it

Sometimes seminars and tutorials can be very quiet, especially at the beginning of a course when many students are not yet comfortable in a group setting. But later, when the setting feels more familiar, the discussions may become very lively. It can be difficult to get a chance to speak, as everybody seems to have something to say. You might find that the same two or three students seem to talk the most and dominate each seminar. So how can you get a chance?

Lecturers try to make seminars and tutorials fairly relaxed and friendly. However, as they are still quite formal and respectful occasions, direct interruptions are not very common. It is therefore important to listen carefully so you can identify an opportunity for a change of turn.

Exercise 5

01

Listen to two students talking in a seminar. First one speaks, then the other. When does the change of turn happen? Do you think the first speaker had finished speaking? Had she said everything she wanted to say?

It is a very common for a change of turn to happen at the end of a sentence in this way. Speakers wait for opportunities like this to take their turn to speak. Interruptions in the middle of a sentence are less common.

In some cultures, interrupting in the middle of a sentence may be more common. So you should try to be aware of the conventions of speaking in the country where you are studying and try to follow them.

Tips

✓ Another useful technique to find an opportunity for a change of turn is to make clear eye contact with the person speaking, the lecturer, or the person leading the seminar. By making eye contact, you can indicate that you wish to speak. You can also raise your hand slightly to support this. You may find that the speaker then turns their attention to you, as they are about to finish.

✓ Listen for phrases like 'you know' and 'something like that', as these often signal that a speaker has finished.

Preventing interruptions

So, you have learned how to get a chance to speak. But how can you make sure you get to finish what you want to say before another change of turn takes place? How can you prevent others from interrupting you?

Exercise 6

02

Read and listen to the sentences below. Match the sentences, 1–3, with a–c, the techniques the speakers use to protect themselves from an interruption.

1 One thing I found interesting was that 80 per cent of the country's income goes to 20 per cent of the population, and I also think the debt problems that were described were important.	a The speaker begins by saying how many things she intends to say.
2 There were a couple of things I found interesting – how the international system is basically anarchic, and also how the main goal of all states is survival …	b The speaker uses a subordinating word (words like 'if', 'because', 'since' and 'when'); this shows that she wants to give two pieces of information.
3 I think that because Machiavelli wrote *The Prince* just for one reader and that we don't even know if he was being satirical or not, it's important not to make too many judgements about his morality.	c The speaker uses a coordinating word (words like 'but', 'or' and 'and') to show that she has something more to say.

Glossary

prevent
To prevent something means to ensure that it does not happen.

Note that using a coordinating word to prevent interruption is not always effective because people sometimes understand these words to be signals that they can interrupt and start speaking. One study found that nearly a third of all changes of turn happened after coordinating words.

Once you are speaking, it is important to make the best of the opportunity because – as you saw above – other students may also be waiting for a chance to participate. You can use your chance well by making several points and asking several questions at the same time.

For example:

In terms of the manufacturing process, I'd be interested to know how much the technology is able to respond to the manufacturing needs; where the materials come from; and whether it's the manufacturers who ask for new materials or the suppliers who suggest them.

2 Seminars and tutorials

If you are still interrupted, use the following useful phrases to try and get another turn, so you can finish the point you were making.

> **Finishing what you were saying**
>
> Just to finish what I was saying before, ...
> That's true, but what I wanted to say was ...
> Can I just finish what I was saying before?

Getting information

Glossary

method
A method is a particular way of doing something.

Remember, one of the most important things about seminars and tutorials is that they can be a good opportunity to check and clarify things and to ask questions. Of course, to get information you can ask a simple question. However, there are other methods you can use, which are common in seminars.

It is quite common to justify a request for information. Use the following useful phrases to do this.

> **Justifying a request**
>
> **I was wondering,** how would this kind of thing affect a country's exports?
> **I'm just curious if** the temples also had an economic function.
> **Just out of interest,** how much was Verdi influenced by Meyerbeer?

It is also common to link back your request for information to something that was said earlier.

> **Linking to an earlier contribution**
>
> Earlier you said ...
> You mentioned before that ...
> Just thinking about your previous point, ...

Presenting

It is always a good idea when you ask for information, to confirm what you have already understood. By doing this, you show your lecturer and the other students that you are listening and following what is being said. This will make you feel more confident about what you already know and when you request that something be repeated or explained, your request will seem reasonable.

So, instead of just saying 'Can you repeat that, please?', it is better to use the useful phrases below.

Asking for more information about what you have understood

Could you expand on what you mean when you say …?
Can you just explain why …?
You say that … . How does this …?
When you say …, what exactly do you mean?
Could you just repeat the point about …?

It can be even more effective to try and paraphrase something to check that it is correct. You can use phrases like these.

Paraphrasing

So do you mean that …?
So does the writer mean that …?

So you're saying that …?
So what the writer is saying is that …?

So in other words, …
So the point is that …

You can practise these useful phrases while doing your set reading or reading your lecture notes, in preparation for a seminar. Practise asking the lecturer about specific things you do not understand well. Write out what you plan to say and practise it aloud or imagine the conversation in your head.

Exercise 7

Read the short text below, or choose some lecture notes or other material from your course. Imagine you are in a seminar. Practise checking your understanding by paraphrasing the main ideas of what you read in the text.

Partly as a result of this dictatorship of vested interests, partly through corruption and misrule, and the inequality and destructiveness of an economic system which depends for its survival on the issue of endless debt, the prosperity perpetually promised by the rich world to the poor perpetually fails to materialize. Almost half of the world's population lives on less than two dollars a day; one fifth on less than one. Despite a global surplus of food, 840 million people are officially classified as malnourished, as they lack the money required to buy it.

Tip ✓ It is very common to start speaking by stating the topic that you are going to talk about.

E.g. *Your idea for the advertising campaign – can you explain why you chose to ignore radio advertising?*

There is normally a short pause after the topic is stated. This kind of structure would be considered incorrect in written language, but it is very common in speaking. It helps to make it immediately clear what you are going to talk about.

Agreeing and disagreeing

The practice of agreeing and disagreeing with other people is an important feature of seminars or tutorials. It is common to add some of your own ideas when you say you agree. Use the following useful phrases to add your own thoughts.

> **Agreeing and adding your thoughts**
>
> I agree with that because …
> I think that's true for another reason …
> Yeah, and also because …

When you disagree in seminars and tutorials, it is advisable to use different techniques to make what you say a little indirect, as it is not appropriate to make very strong statements. Do Exercise 8 to practise some different ways of doing this.

Exercise 8

Look at the sentences below. In each one, the speaker is disagreeing indirectly. Match the underlined parts, 1–4, to the techniques, a–d.

1 Not all of the Millennium Development Goals are easy to achieve, <u>though</u>.	**a** agreeing first, but then making a contrasting statement
2 <u>That's true, but</u> I also think the other treatment options are important.	**b** asking a negative question
3 <u>Don't you think</u> that governments should invest more during periods like this?	**c** using a question tag (a question at the end of a sentence)
4 Companies like this don't have much chance of success, <u>do they</u>?	**d** using a word to show a contrast

Giving a seminar paper

In the rest of this chapter, you will learn about seminar papers. As explained at the beginning of this chapter, giving a seminar paper normally involves doing some set reading and possibly preparing a paper in advance. In the seminar, you should talk about what you have read or the work you have done. This presentation is often followed by a discussion in which the lecturer and all the students participate.

Exercise 9

Listen to somebody beginning to present a seminar paper. What two things does she do?

03

There is quite a lot of variation in exactly how seminar papers are given. Sometimes students are asked to prepare a written paper which they should then read in the seminar. Alternatively, you might find that everyone reads from notes. Students often feel it is more difficult to read from notes than to read a paper aloud. However, the people listening will find it much easier and more interesting to listen to somebody speaking from notes than to someone reading aloud from a script.

In this section, you will look at how to improve your performance when you have to read from a text. If you are unsure about whether you need to read from a text or to speak from notes, ask your lecturer and observe what other students do.

For more information on making and using notes, see Chapter 4.

For more information on making and using notes, see Chapter 4.

Glossary

emphasize
To emphasize something means to indicate that it is particularly important or true, or to draw special attention to it.

It is much easier to read a written text than to listen to someone reading it aloud. When we speak naturally, we pause a lot, repeat important points and refer back to points we have already mentioned. These pauses and repetitions help the people listening to understand us. When we write a text, we know that our readers can stop reading to think about an important point or reread certain sections. This means that when we write, we do not need to repeat ourselves to make a point clear. However, if you read aloud a written text, the people listening are not able to do any of these things and may find it difficult to follow. So, it is important to find techniques, such as emphasizing key words, to make the experience easier for your listeners.

Exercise 10
Listen to a text being read. How easy did you find it to follow?

04

Exercise 11
Listen to the text being read again. Did you find it easier to follow this time? Why?

Below is the text that the speaker reads from. The key words are underlined and there are some lines to show where to make pauses. Since the speaker made these pauses and emphasized the key words, it is easier to understand him reading it.

05

The <u>biggest impact</u> | on the newspaper business model | has been the <u>difference</u> between reading news on a <u>daily</u> basis | versus having a <u>continual updating stream</u> of news available | for free | on the <u>internet</u>. By the time a <u>newspaper</u> arrives at your front door | in the <u>morning</u>|, you have probably <u>already read</u> about the <u>earthquake</u> in <u>Asia</u> or the latest <u>political scandal</u> in Washington DC. <u>Furthermore</u>, along with <u>traditional</u> online news outlets | like newspaper websites |, people are turning to <u>alternative</u> online sources, for example, reading <u>political blogs</u> | rather than political coverage in the <u>paper.</u>

Source: Tancer, Bill (2009). *Click: What We Do Online and Why It Matters*. London: HarperCollins.

Exercise 12

Look at the following text, which is a continuation of the text you have just read and listened to. In the first sentence, the key words are underlined and the pauses are marked. Underline the key words and insert vertical lines where you think pauses are necessary in the rest of the paragraph. Then read it aloud. Record yourself if you can.

> What can an <u>industry do</u> | when <u>all</u> of its value | is in the process of being <u>replaced</u> by a resource that is <u>almost free</u> | to the <u>consumer</u>? Most newspapers have responded by adapting to the new reality, offering as much up-to-date news on their websites, changing their business model to rely increasingly on internet advertising revenue instead of sales and print advertising. Some papers have gone further, deciding to adapt to the more interactive nature of the internet and allowing readers to participate by commenting on articles or even writing new articles. But for some newspapers, this strategy has not been totally successful.

You can do exactly the same thing with the text you need to read as a seminar paper. Make sure you practise reading your text aloud before you go to the seminar. Reading silently is not normally good enough practice, so it is best to find somewhere you can practise reading aloud where you will not feel embarrassed or be disturbed. If you can, ask a friend or another student to listen to you and ask them for feedback on your performance.

Tips   ✓   Print out your presentation in a larger font size than usual (14 or 16), with 1.5 or double spacing. This will make it easier to read and will give you space in which to mark the key words and pauses.

      ✓   If you have to give a seminar paper, you will probably need to respond to other students' questions at the end.

For more information on asking for and answering questions, see Chapters 3 and 11.

Remember

✓ Find out the kinds of tutorials and seminars you will take part in.

✓ Find out if you need to do any presentations.

✓ Make sure you prepare well for seminars by reading actively and identifying topics you agree with or want to discuss.

✓ Express yourself without making statements that are too emphatic.

✓ Listen for the right time to take your turn to speak.

✓ Ask questions by trying to show what you already understand.

✓ Disagree indirectly with other people's opinions.

✓ If you have to read a seminar paper to an audience, help them by slowing down at key points and taking plenty of pauses.

3 | Planning and structuring formal presentations

Aims ✓ think about the brief for your presentation   ✓ give the main part of a presentation and move from part to part

✓ structure a presentation

✓ give introductions and conclusions to your presentation

Aims

 Quiz
Self-evaluation

Read the statements, then circle the word which is true for you.

1	I understand how to analyse the brief and the purpose of a presentation.	agree | disagree | not sure
2	I know the basic structure of a presentation.	agree | disagree | not sure
3	I know what to include in introductions and conclusions.	agree | disagree | not sure
4	I know the right kinds of phrases to use in different parts of a presentation.	agree | disagree | not sure

Thinking about the brief and the purpose of your presentation

Glossary

content
If you refer to the content or contents of something such as a book, speech, or television programme, you are referring to the subject that it deals with, or the ideas that it expresses.

As discussed in Chapter 1, during your studies you might be asked to give different types of presentations and for different reasons. It is important that you read and think carefully about the brief you are given for your presentation. The content you choose for your presentation will depend on several things.

First, you need to think about the instructions you get from your lecturer. You might be given a question to answer or a topic to talk about; alternatively, you might be asked to do a literature review or discuss a statement. Perhaps you will need to do a combination of some of these tasks. Whatever your brief, first think about how you can 'narrow it down' – in other words, how to identify a particular area within your brief to focus on. In an oral presentation, you may only have enough time to provide a limited amount of information, with limited detail.

For example, imagine you are a business studies student. You are required to do a ten-minute presentation on this question: 'In what ways has the financial crisis affected business in the USA?'

In ten minutes, you cannot answer the question fully. In this case, it would be better for you to focus on a specific aspect of the question (e.g. automobile exports or the banking sector). Often, you will find that the more specific the topic you choose, the better your presentation is.

Exercise 1

Imagine you have to give a ten-minute oral presentation on the following topic: 'Outline some challenges facing the education sector in a country you are familiar with and suggest how they could be overcome.'

Try to narrow the question down, by identifying a specific area to focus on.

Glossary

literature review
If you do a literature review, you read relevant literature, such as books and journal articles so that you have a good, basic knowledge of a particular topic.

When you are given a question to answer in your presentation, you need to narrow down the topic. You could do this by first doing a literature review and your own analysis. In your presentation, you could talk about your answer and how you reached it.

If you are only given a topic to discuss, instead of a question, you should focus on one or a few specific areas relating to it. You may benefit from choosing what you find most interesting about the topic, as this will make your preparation more enjoyable and interesting too. Make sure that what you speak about is relevant to the brief. Do not include anything that is not directly relevant. Make sure that your whole presentation leads to a clear response to the brief.

Tips
✓ It is a good idea to check with your lecturer that your presentation focus is acceptable. Write a rough outline and ask if your lecturer can check it quickly in your next seminar. They may prefer to receive it by email.
✓ Be sure you know how long your presentation should last. Find out how much time you will have and if it includes questions at the end.

For more information about timing, look at Chapter 5.

Audience

Your audience is also part of your brief, as your audience will affect what you choose to say and how you say it. You will probably give a presentation to your seminar group, so the audience will be other students and your lecturer. However, especially if you are a postgraduate, you might be expected to present your research to other researchers and lecturers. When you prepare your presentation, think about the following three areas.

- Consider the audience when you define your topic. First, you need to think about what they may already know. There is no point in presenting information that has already been covered in previous lectures or seminars or that the audience already knows from their own research. At the same time, you cannot expect students to remember everything that has been covered in their studies. Think about revising important points that are relevant to your presentation.

- Be careful when you use terminology. When you read about a topic and become knowledgeable about it, its terminology becomes familiar to you. It is easy to forget that others may not know as much as you do. Try to remember what you knew and did not know before you started working on your presentation. Then assume that your audience will probably have the knowledge level you had before you started so you may need to explain any terminology you use.

- Put yourself in the audience's place and think about what they might want.

Imagine you were in the audience on the day of the presentation and think about what you would like to learn from the presentation. Set yourself clear goals and objectives about what you would like your audience to learn. What new knowledge would you like them to leave with?

Remember that overall you are presenting *to* an audience and who exactly is in the audience should make a difference to what you choose to say.

Thinking about assessment

Another aspect of your brief is how your presentation will be assessed. There are many different ways a presentation can be assessed and your lecturer may even use a personal marking scheme with criteria for different aspects of your presentation.

You will probably be assessed on both the content of your presentation (in other words, the quality of your academic work) and on how you give the presentation (your presenting skills).

Ask your lecturer if you can see a copy of the assessment criteria that they will use. You might discover that more marks are given for some aspects than for others. Knowing this will help you choose what to concentrate on when preparing your preparation. Your lecturer may not use different criteria, but may give you a single mark. In this case, you can still ask for guidance on what they consider important in a presentation. For example, your lecturer might say that that how you structure and organize your presentation is more important than your visual aids. Knowing this, you can focus on those features, instead of spending a lot of time on visual aids.

Deciding what content to include

Once you have done a thorough analysis of the brief and have decided what exactly you want to concentrate on, start thinking in more detail about what to include. At this stage, you should think about what you already know about the topic. You can do this by looking back at any reading you have done on the topic or at your lecture notes. At this point, you could do some basic research. However, avoid reading in too much detail, because you need to keep a general view of the topic area.

Next, make a list of all the things you might want to talk about – this list does not need to be organized or ordered. Then look at your list and organize your ideas into sections; under each section, there should be at least two or three main points. Now that you have identified your sections, do some more detailed reading and research to finalize your content. You might decide to make some changes to the content at this stage.

Exercise 2

Put the following preparation stages in order from 1–7, according to what you have learned.

- ☐ **a** make a list of all your ideas
- ☐ **b** review what you already know
- ☐ **c** do some basic research
- ☐ **d** organize your ideas into sections
- ☐ **e** make any final changes
- 1 **f** analyse the brief and decide on your focus
- ☐ **g** do more detailed research

How should you organize the main part of your presentation? This will depend on what you talk about – there are no strict rules. Think about how to divide what you want to say into sections. Typically, a student presentation lasting ten to twenty minutes should be divided into between three and ten main sections. Each section should contain at least one main point, which is clearly relevant to the topic. Remember that you should have clear aims for your presentation and each section should relate to them.

Exercise 3

Imagine you need to give a ten-minute presentation on this topic: 'Describe an educational system with which you are familiar and summarize its strengths and weaknesses.'

Organize the list of ideas below into three sections. Create a heading for each section.

- three types of school: primary school, middle school, high school
- school leavers have good writing and mathematics skills
- the age at which you go to school and university
- focus on learning facts
- does not develop analytical skills
- types of university
- frequent examinations
- focus on basic skills, like reading, writing and mathematics
- does not provide much preparation for the workplace

Exercise 4

Look at appendix 4, 'A presentation outline', on pages 164 and 165. You can use it to help you plan your presentation.

Basic structure

The basic structure for any presentation should be:

- saying what you are going to say (the introduction),

- saying it (the main part of the presentation),

- saying what you said (the conclusion).

Although this sounds a bit repetitive, this is what is expected in an academic presentation. By saying what you are going to say, you prepare your audience. It is easier to follow and understand a presentation if you know what is coming. When you say what you have said, you summarize and bring all your points together. This is important, because you want the audience to have a clear idea of how everything you said fits together. You need to help them with this process.

This structure is very simplistic, but all presentations follow the same basic pattern. You will now learn about the structure in more detail.

Introductions

The main purpose of your introduction is to tell your audience what you are going to talk about. However, introductions often include a number of other features.

Exercise 5

Listen to the introduction to a presentation about exports from the developing world. Number the features in the order that you hear them.

06

☐	**a**	presenter gives structure of presentation
☐	**b**	presenter introduces herself
☐	**c**	presenter gives an interesting fact to get the audience's interest
1	**d**	presenter welcomes audience
☐	**e**	presenter introduces the topic

Exercise 6

Look at the following useful phrases you can use in the introduction of a presentation. You heard some of the phrases in Exercise 5. Listen to the phrases and write in the missing words.

Introducing yourself

I'm …

My name's …

Introducing the topic

The topic _____ _____ _____ _____ _____ today is …

This morning I'm going to _____ _____ …

Today I'm going to _____ and _____ …

Getting the audience interested

One thing _____ _____ _____ _____ about … is

Did you _____ _____ …?

Have you ever _____ _____ why …?

Giving the structure of your presentation

I'm _____ going to … / _____ I'm going to … / _____ , I'm going to …

I'm going to __ __ looking at … / Then I'll __ __ to … / __ __, I'll talk to you about …

My presentation _____ _____ _____ three parts. First, … / Second, … / Third, …

The main part of the presentation

The content of your presentation will depend on the subject you are studying and your specific topic. As you know, it is important to divide your presentation into clear sections. It is equally important to indicate to your audience when you move from one of these sections to another. So, once you finish your introduction, you should indicate clearly that you are moving on to the first section of the main part of your presentation. Do the same when you move from one section to the next, in the main part of the presentation. To do this, you can use 'signposting' language, which shows your audience where they are going. Now look at Exercise 7 for some phrases you can use to indicate the start of a new section of a presentation.

Exercise 7

Read the four excerpts from a presentation about exports from countries in the developing world. The phrases in **bold** show you where a new section starts. Listen to the audio track and repeat the phrases in bold.

08

1   … finally, I'll look at the positive effects that even a small increase on exports could have on developing nations. **So, moving on to** the kinds of goods exported by developing countries in Africa and Asia, …

2   … so you can see the kinds of products that are typically available for export. **Let's turn to** the kinds of the restrictions countries in the developing world have to deal with, perhaps the first thing to say is …

3   … and that's why countries in the developing world continue to have problems. **Let's look now at** what would happen if countries in the developing world were able to increase their exports.

4   **I'd like to conclude by** reviewing the three areas I looked at in this presentation.

In the main part of your presentation, you may need to refer to sources you have used in your research. The language you use to mention sources is similar to that used in essay writing. However, presentations are less formal than essays, so there are some differences.

Exercise 8

Read the following useful phrases which can be used to refer to sources. Which of the phrases can you use only in a presentation? Which phrases are suitable for both, a presentation and an essay?

Referring to sources

According to …,

X says that …

X argues that …

X's theory is that …

Here you can see X's definition of …

Conclusions

You have learned about introductions (saying what you are going to say) and the main part of the presentation (saying it). In your conclusion, it is important that you summarize the content of the presentation (saying what you said). Your conclusion should be quite similar to your introduction. Do not worry about the fact that you are repeating yourself, because this is expected in an academic presentation. By repeating the main points of your presentation, you reinforce them for your audience and you bring everything together. However, it is important that you do not introduce any new ideas in your conclusion. Always remember that the conclusion is your chance to summarize what you have spoken about, not to give new information.

As with introductions, you may want to include some other features, too. You will learn about this in Exercise 9.

Tip ✓ Make sure you end your presentation confidently. If you are expected to answer questions, then ask if there are any, using a confident voice. If not, you can thank the audience for their time and attention.

Exercise 9

Listen to the conclusion to the presentation about exports from countries in the developing world. Write 1–5 next to the following features, according to the order in which you hear them.

- [ ] **a** saying what the main argument or conclusion of the presentation was
- [ ] **b** thanking the audience
- [ ] **c** asking if there are any questions
- [1] **d** repeating the main points
- [ ] **e** leaving the audience with an interesting thought or idea

While it is common to answer questions at the end of a presentation, you might not be expected to in your course. Check with your lecturer if you are uncertain.

Exercise 10

Look at the headings (a–d) and match them to the correct phrases (1–4).

a Asking for questions	**1** In conclusion, we looked at ... I'd like to conclude by reviewing ...
b Thanking the audience	**2** And I argued that ... I hoped to show that ...
c Repeating the main points	**3** Are there any questions? Does anybody have a question?
d Saying what the main argument or conclusion was	**4** Thank you for listening. Thanks for your attention.

Exercise 11

There are many different ways you could leave the audience with an interesting thought or idea. Match the techniques, 1–3, with the examples, a–c.

1 asking the audience a question	**a** The important thing for us to think about now is how we can improve the situation in the coming decades.
2 showing or reading a quotation	**b** So, what would you do if you were a policy-maker in the EU?
3 making a reference to the future	**c** I'd like to finish by reading you a quotation from Keynes.

Speaking as part of a group

It is common for universities to expect their students to give group presentations, in addition to individual ones. While everything you have learned in this chapter applies equally to individual and group presentations, there are also some extra things to think about.

Your first task may be to form a group. Sometimes the lecturer decides on the groups, but normally students are expected to form groups themselves. When choosing people to work with, try to choose people who you have a good relationship with and who you can meet up with easily. It needs to be easy for you to stay in contact with each other.

Once you have decided on your group, you will need to analyse your brief together. Then, as a group, go through the process described in Exercise 2 to decide on your content. Once you have agreed on the content, you can decide on who is going to do what. Even if you need to do a lot of research individually, you need to stay in contact with the other people in your group. If you are in a group of three, for example, you need to make sure that you prepare a single presentation, presented by three people, and not three different mini-presentations.

Introductions, conclusions and moving from part to part in a group

Introductions in a group are very similar to what you have already learned about. First, you need to decide which member of the group will give the introduction – usually, only one person does this. You may want to choose one of the most confident speakers to give the introduction, so that you make a good first impression and immediately get your audience's attention.

In an introduction to a group presentation, the speaker should introduce all the members of the group, one by one, not just himself or herself. When telling the audience about the content of the presentation, the speaker should say who is going to talk about each area, for example: 'After the introduction, Juan is going to talk about USPs. Next, Sharief will explain … '. When one speaker finishes their section, instead of just saying what topic will come next, the speaker also needs to say who will talk about it.

Exercise 12

Listen to some phrases from a presentation. Put the words in the correct order.

10

1   Now Sara about / going / is / talk / to _____

2   Next, Mehmet on / to / move / will _____

3   Xu Li going / is / at / now / to / look _____

> **Tip** ✓ Each group member needs to know what the others are planning to say. Make sure you know what the person speaking before you has planned, especially when they introduce you. Make sure that they introduce you and explain what you will talk about correctly. Likewise, check with the person you are going to introduce that what you plan to say is accurate.

The person who gives the conclusion to your group presentation should be a confident speaker. There is nothing wrong with the same person doing the introduction and conclusion. However, if each student is assessed individually for their presentation, instead of everyone receiving the same mark, it may be fairer if the introduction and conclusion are given by different speakers. Again, the person giving the conclusion summarizes *who* said what, not just *what* was said.

When working in groups, you need to be careful about how you will move around during your presentation. Think about where the other members of the group will sit or stand when they are not speaking. They should be out of the way, so that the audience is focused only on the current speaker. The members of the group should know where to go when they have finished speaking, to make space for the new speaker.

For more information on practical matters, see Chapter 10.

Remember

✓ Think about your brief and make your topic as specific as possible.

✓ Think about your audience.

✓ Think about how you will be assessed.

✓ Do your research systematically. Start by thinking about what you already know, then decide on basic sections for your presentation, and then do more detailed reading.

✓ Say what you are going to say, say it and say what you said.

✓ Use different techniques to make your introduction and conclusion effective.

✓ Use signposting phrases to help your audience understand the organization of your presentation.

✓ If you are giving a group presentation, instead of an individual one, think about what needs to be done differently.

4 | Making and using notes

Aims
- ✓ understand some differences between spoken and written English
- ✓ understand why it is important to speak from notes
- ✓ make notes
- ✓ understand some practical considerations of speaking from notes

Aims

? Quiz
Self-evaluation

Read the statements, then circle the word which is true for you.

1	I know some basic differences between spoken and written English.	agree | disagree | not sure
2	I know why it is important to speak from notes in a presentation.	agree | disagree | not sure
3	I know what to include when making notes.	agree | disagree | not sure
4	I feel confident speaking from notes.	agree | disagree | not sure

Differences between spoken and written English

When students are asked to prepare a presentation for the first time, many immediately think about writing a script to read aloud. Presenting like this is not a good idea, however. In Chapter 3, you learned that it is easier to read a written text alone than to listen to it being read aloud. This is because when you are reading, you can pause to think about an important point, you can read certain sections again and again and you can go back to check what was written earlier. Since you can use none of these techniques when someone is reading to you, it is more difficult to follow what they are saying. When people speak naturally – even in a presentation – they pause, repeat things and refer back to what they said before. This makes it easier for other people to understand what is being said.

Look at some more differences between spoken and written English in Exercise 1.

Exercise 1

Read the following list of features of language. If the sentence describes a feature of spoken English, write an S next to it. If the feature described is of written English, write a W.

1   nouns and verbs are used in equal number

2   long noun phrases are used frequently (e.g. *The questionnaire, which was sent out in May and completed by over 10,000 respondents from all over the country*, revealed some interesting trends.)

3   first and second personal pronouns ('I', 'me', 'we', 'us', and 'you') are much more common

4   grammar words (e.g. auxiliary verbs, prepositions and articles) are used more frequently

5   the range of vocabulary is smaller

Glossary

by heart
If you know something such as a poem by heart, you have learned it so well that you can remember it without having to read it.

commonplace
If something is commonplace, it happens often or is often found, and is therefore not surprising.

You can see that there are several differences between spoken and written language. When you give a presentation, you will not be expected to speak informally, as if chatting with a friend. However, if you write a text and read it aloud as your presentation, you will use language features that are not appropriate in a spoken context and those features will make it difficult for others to understand you.

The same is true if you write a script and then learn it 'by heart' – a technique which is used by many students from educational backgrounds where learning by heart is commonplace. In this case, even though you are not reading from a script, the language of the text you write and memorize will not be appropriate for the spoken context of a university presentation. It will probably sound too formal and use the features of written English rather than the features of spoken English.

Speaking from notes

You have learned that when you give a presentation, you should not read a text aloud. To give a presentation without reading a prepared text, you first need to know the content of your presentation well. If you have researched the topic thoroughly and organized your ideas into sections, as described in Chapter 3, you should be fairly confident about what you want to say. However, you will probably find it difficult to remember everything, especially when you are under the pressure of presenting to an audience. This means that you need to create some notes to speak from – these notes will help you remember what you want to say.

Tip ✓ Although you should use notes for most of your presentation, it can be a good idea to write out the first two or three sentences of your introduction in full. If you are feeling nervous at the beginning, you will be glad to have the sentences to read aloud. Then you can continue speaking from your notes.

Notes should contain the basic information you wish to present, but should not contain full sentences to read out. The easiest way to use notes is to create prompt cards – small pieces of paper you hold and refer to during your presentation.

For example:

> _USA_
>
> _definition different: top speed = 180–240 km/h_
> _high-speed rail becoming more attractive:_
>   _high fuel prices_
>   _airport security_
>   _environmental concerns_
> _2009: 8 bn dollars for high-speed rail_
>   _10 strategic corridors_

Exercise 2

Read the following information from the presentation about high-speed rail in the USA.

The USA has a slightly different definition of high-speed rail. While in Europe the term is usually used to refer to trains that reach a minimum speed of 250 kilometres per hour, in the USA the speeds are generally lower, from 180 to 240 kilometres per hour.

High-speed rail is becoming more attractive to Americans, for a number of reasons. Firstly, high fuel prices have pushed up the cost of travelling by plane and by car, long the preferred means of transport for longer journeys within the United States. Travelling by plane has also lost some of its allure, with increased airport security increasing journey times and making the experience less pleasant than previously. Finally, there is now more awareness of the environmental costs of travelling by car or by plane.

It appears that the federal government is keen to invest in the railways. In 2009, Congress allocated $8 billion to rail projects, a large part of which is to be spent on high-speed rail. In the same year, the Federal Railroad Administration (FRA) published a plan identifying ten key rail corridors, where high-speed rail is to be developed and other upgrades made to existing lines.

Now look back at the notes you read earlier and compare them to the text, to make sure you understand them. Practise presenting the information aloud. Use the notes, but do not look at the original text. If possible, record yourself and listen to your recording.

Exercise 3

Listen to a presenter speak from the prompt card on page 42. Compare the recording to your own performance.

11

How easy did you find this exercise? If you were confident that you had understood the information in the original text, you should not have found it too difficult. When you do your own presentation, you will naturally feel more comfortable and knowledgeable about your content and it should not be too difficult to speak from notes.

Making notes

Look again at the notes you read in Exercise 2. Did you notice that only the most important words and information from the text appeared in them? When you make notes, try to limit how many words you write. This will make your notes easier to use when you are speaking. You will also speak more naturally if you are reading a small number of words than if you write out longer phrases and sentences. Do Exercise 4 to practise writing notes.

Exercise 4

Read the following text about the International Space Station and make notes on it. Use the notes you saw on page 42 to guide you. Remember to include only the most important information.

The International Space Station is a manned station in orbit around the Earth. It orbits at 240 statute miles, travelling at 17,500 miles an hour and is the result of cooperation between five space agencies and 16 countries. The first crew arrived in November 2000 and since then there has been a continuous human presence on board; when fully crewed, it hosts six astronauts.

The station is essentially a research laboratory where experiments are conducted in a number of different areas, including future technologies, new materials, medical research and communications technology. It may eventually also be used as a base for missions to the Moon, Mars and asteroids.

One common misconception about the International Space Station is that there is little gravity – in fact, the gravitational pull of the Earth is only slightly weaker on the station than on the surface of the Earth. The apparent weightlessness is actually caused by the fact that the station is constantly falling towards the Earth, like everything in orbit.

Exercise 5

Practise speaking from the notes that you wrote for Exercise 4. Record yourself if possible. Then listen to your recording and assess your performance.

Practical considerations

Glossary

durable
Something that
is durable is
strong and lasts
a long time
without breaking
or becoming
weaker.

disadvantage
A disadvantage
is a factor which
makes someone
or something
less useful,
acceptable, or
successful than
other people or
things.

The notes you read and wrote were in boxes of this size: 152 mm wide by 102 mm high (6 inches by 4 inches). This is the standard size for 'index cards', which you can buy from stationery shops. You may find index cards perfect for writing your notes on for a presentation. They are the right size, big enough to fit the content you need, but small enough to force you to focus on the most important information. Index cards are made of light cardboard, so they are durable and easy to hold in one hand. Your notes will probably not be perfect the first time you make them. As you practise and do more thorough research, your notes will improve so you might want to do the first drafts on paper. Then, when you have finalized your preparation, write your final notes on prompt cards.

If you cannot find index cards or do not wish to use them, you can use normal paper. The disadvantage of paper is that it is thinner than index cards and not as easy to hold. Several sheets of paper held together can be noisy, especially if you are feeling nervous.

Tips

✓ If you only have access to A4 or letter-sized paper for your notes, cut the paper in half. A whole sheet of paper may be too big – it will be very noticeable to your audience and may tempt you to write too much on each piece.

✓ While preparing your notes, number each card or piece of paper at the bottom, in the order you will use them. In this way, if your notes get mixed up – for example, if you drop them – their numbering will help you find your place again.

✓ If you are using PowerPoint presentation software for your visual aids (see Chapters 8 and 9), you can make notes directly in the software and print out a summary of your slides. While this is a good way of keeping everything together, your print-out will probably be on A4 or letter-sized paper, which has the disadvantages mentioned earlier.

In addition to your notes, you can also write other useful things on your cards or pieces of paper.

Exercise 6

Look at the following prompt card. What information has the student included, in addition to his main notes?

USA

definition different: top speed = 180–240 km/h

high-speed rail becoming more attractive:

    high fuel prices

    airport security

    environmental concerns

2009: 8 bn dollars for high-speed rail

    10 strategic corridors

SLOW DOWN!

MAKE EYE CONTACT   *CHANGE SLIDE*

Your notes are an excellent place to put extra information like this. Take care not to write too much, as you will find it hard to read them while you are presenting.

Practising with notes

Glossary

unobtrusively
If you describe
something or
someone as
unobtrusive, you
mean that they
are not easily
noticed or do not
draw attention
to themselves.

glance
If you glance at
something or
someone, you
look at them
very quickly
and then look
away again
immediately.

When you are nervous, as you might be during your presentation, even simple things like holding notes can become difficult. It is worth taking the time to focus specifically on the practical side of speaking from notes.

If possible, practise speaking from your notes in front of a long mirror. This way, you can see how your audience will see you. Try to hold your notes as low as possible – they need to be high enough so you can read them, but should not hide your face. Practise changing from one prompt card or piece of paper to the next; try to do it quickly and unobtrusively. You should try to maintain eye contact (with yourself in the mirror) as much as possible. Instead of reading from your cards, glance down at them. Try to speak from your notes and change from card to card without looking down for too long.

Remember

✓ There are important differences between spoken and written English.

✓ Reading aloud a written text for a presentation is not advisable. Instead, speak from notes.

✓ When you take notes, include only the most important words and information. Do not write full sentences, apart from the first two or three from the introduction to give yourself confidence.

✓ Use prompt cards to write your notes on.

✓ You can include other useful information on your notes, to help you during your presentation.

✓ Practise the practical side of speaking from notes in front of a mirror.

5 | Using your voice

Aims ✓ control your breathing
✓ find the right volume and pace
✓ use intonation to make your message clear

✓ learn about word stress and sentence stress
✓ make your presentation more fluent

Aims

? Quiz
Self-evaluation

Read the statements, then circle the word which is true for you.

1	I know how to control my breathing.	agree | disagree | not sure
2	I feel confident about how loudly I speak.	agree | disagree | not sure
3	I know how to control the pace (speed) of my voice.	agree | disagree | not sure
4	I know how to vary the tone of my voice to make my message clear.	agree | disagree | not sure
5	I understand the importance of stressing (emphasizing) words and which words to stress in a sentence.	agree | disagree | not sure
6	I know how to use weak forms and to join words together to make my speech fluent.	agree | disagree | not sure

Using your voice in a presentation

Glossary

highlight
If someone or something highlights a point or problem, they emphasize it or make you think about it.

Your voice is essential to your presentation. It is the main tool you have to communicate, so you need to learn how to use it as effectively as possible. In addition to communicating your basic message, your voice can also highlight important parts of your presentation and improve the clarity of your message. Of course, if your first language is not English, nobody expects you to sound like a native speaker. However, there are many techniques you can learn to improve your performance.

Breathing

Breathing is fundamental to how you sound when you speak. Of course, everybody knows how to breathe. When you give a presentation, your voice needs to be louder than normal and you need use your voice to support your communication. To do this well, you need to learn some basic control of your breathing.

When we speak, we exhale air from our lungs and simultaneously contract our vocal cords. The cords vibrate and this produces sound. To change this sound, we use different parts of our bodies, such as our tongues and mouths, but everything starts with the air we have in our lungs. The more air you can store in your lungs when you breathe in, the better control you will have of your breathing and your voice.

Tip ✓ Take a bottle of water with you on the day of your presentation. Drink some before you start speaking to make sure your vocal cords are moist and keep the bottle near you during your presentation. It is advisable *not* to drink during your presentation, as this can stop the audience from focusing. However, it is useful to have the bottle there for an emergency, for example, if your throat feels dry or you start coughing.

Exercise 1

Take a deep breath – breathe in as much air as possible. Feel the air fill your shoulders, your chest, and your abdomen. Then breathe out slowly, releasing the air slowly and evenly. While you are exhaling, hum (to make a continuous sound with your lips closed). Time yourself using your watch or phone to see how long you can hum for before you run out of breath. Repeat this exercise often, timing yourself, and see if you can increase the length of time you can hum.

Breathing deeply and slowly can also help you calm yourself before and during your presentation.

For more information on keeping calm, see Chapter 10.

Volume

How loudly you speak in your presentation is important. Some people have naturally soft voices, while others are naturally loud. If you do not feel confident about speaking in English or about your ideas, you may speak quietly. However, you need to make sure that your voice is loud enough to be effective in your presentation.

Tips ✓ If you are uncertain of whether you voice is loud enough, you can check this by practising in the room where you will do your presentation, or in a similar place, and ask somebody to tell you if your voice is loud enough. Plan to go to the seminar early with some friends, ask them to sit towards the back of the room and then speak to see if they can hear you clearly.

✓ Remember that when a room is full, you may need to speak louder, so be prepared to talk louder than when you were practising.

Exercise 2

If you are having difficulty with the volume of your voice, work on it before your presentation. Play some music and set the volume to approximately the volume of natural conversation. Then read a text aloud – any text – and try to make your voice clear above the music.

Repeat this exercise often. Each time, increase the volume of the music slightly, until you are speaking at the right volume for a presentation.

Tip ✓ At the beginning of each section of your presentation, when you introduce what you are going to say, increase the volume and raise the pitch (how high or low the sound is) of your voice. This signals to the audience that a new section is beginning. When you finish a section, it is also common to decrease the volume and lower the pitch of your voice.

Pace

Glossary

pace
The pace of something is the speed at which it happens or is done.

The pace of your voice is extremely important. Just as people have different natural volumes to their voices, some people speak faster or more slowly than others. People often speak more quickly when they feel nervous or under pressure. It is important to think about the pace of your voice when you do a presentation.

In Chapter 4, you learned that it is better to speak from notes than from a script. But when you speak from notes, it is difficult to prepare a presentation with the exact number of words needed for the time available. However, it is important to practise your presentation so you can decide on the correct pace.

Exercise 3

Look back at the text in Chapter 2, Exercise 11. The text is 93 words long. Imagine this text was part of a presentation. How long would it take to read it aloud to an audience?

Now read the text aloud two or three times. Once you feel familiar with the text, read it aloud at a suitable pace for a presentation and time yourself. How long did you take? Do you think that was the right speed?

People often increase the pace of their voice when they are nervous, such as while giving a presentation. If you have practised speaking at the right speed, you should realize if this happens to you and will know that you have to to slow down.

If you speak from prompt cards (which you learned about in Chapter 4), you can write reminders to yourself to slow down and also write approximately how long you should speak for each card. Then, if you realize you have finished a section more quickly than the time written on the prompt card, you will know to slow down.

Intonation

Intonation is used to give extra meaning to the words you use and can make your message clearer. Intonation is a large area, but there are a few key techniques that you can use easily to improve your presentations and communicate more effectively.

Look at two common intonation patterns in English. These are the most common patterns:

the fall ↘ the voice goes down

the fall-rise ↘↗ the voice goes down, then up

Exercise 4

Listen to the following sentences. What happens to the voice in the underlined parts of the sentences? Choose the correct pattern.

12

1	My presentation is divided into <u>three parts</u>.		a ↘	b ↘↗
2	<u>Firstly</u>, I'll give a summary of the current situation.		a ↘	b ↘↗
3	Now let's look at the <u>graph</u>.		a ↘	b ↘↗
4	At the <u>end of the presentation</u>, I'll give you all a copy of the results.		a ↘	b ↘↗

So, when do we use the fall intonation and when do we use the fall-rise intonation?

Generally, we use the fall intonation ↘ to show that we are giving new information to the audience (or the person we are speaking to). Look again at the intonation of sentences 1 and 3 in Exercise 4. In sentence 1, the audience does not yet know that the presentation is divided into three parts, so this is new information. In sentence 3, the intonation tells us the presenter is now looking at or talking about something new. This new item is the graph.

We use the fall-rise ⌄↗ to indicate information that is shared in some way. This could mean that the information was mentioned earlier, or that the information is considered obvious and that we expect the audience to already know it. So in sentence 2, the word 'Firstly' does not give any new information. It is obvious that if the speaker is just starting the presentation, this is the first thing to be said. The new information in this sentence comes next, 'I'll give a summary of the current situation', and has a falling tone. In sentence 4, the audience already knows that there is a presentation and that it will have an end. Again, the new information comes next, 'I'll give you a copy', with a falling tone.

Knowing the difference between these two tones can help you communicate your message better. Remember that to highlight new information, you should use a falling tone.

Using intonation to sound confident

When you give a presentation, you are in a position of 'power'. Your audience is listening and learning from you, the expert. In this kind of situation, different intonation patterns are used.

Exercise 5

Listen to the two sentences. Sentence 1 is from a conversation between two friends and sentence 2 is from a presentation. Can you hear a difference in intonation between the word 'OK' in the two sentences?

1   OK, let's call her.

2   OK, let's have a look at the results of the survey.

It is common to use a ⌃↘ intonation with words like *OK, now, so, alright* and *right* at the beginning of a new section in a presentation. It helps the audience understand that a new section is beginning. Additionally, it makes the speaker sound confident and authoritative.

Exercise 6

Listen to the following sentences and repeat them. Make sure you use the rise-fall intonation in the first word of each sentence.

14

1 OK, let's move on to the next part.

2 Right, let's turn to the situation in the early part of the year.

3 So, what can we do to solve the problem?

4 Now, let's think about what makes the policy so successful.

Stress

Glossary

suffix
A suffix is a letter or group of letters, for example '-ly' or '-ness', which is added to the end of a word in order to form a different word, often of a different word class. For example, the suffix '-ly' is added to 'quick' to form 'quickly'.

Stress is how we put emphasis on a syllable, to make it more important than other syllables. Normally, we make a stressed syllable louder and slightly higher in pitch than the other syllables around it.

Using stress effectively is important in a presentation for two reasons. First, if you put the stress on the wrong syllable in an individual word, this is an error and may cause confusion in meaning. Second, by stressing particular words in a sentence, you can show which words you consider the most important.

Here are some general rules about stress in individual words:

- most two-syllable nouns and adjectives have the stress on the first syllable, e.g. _student, language, recent, common_

- most two-syllable verbs have the stress on the second syllable, e.g. _present, review, research, explore_

- words that have suffixes like -ial, -ible/-able, -ic(al), -ience/-ient/-iency, -ify, -ion(al), -ious/-eous, -ity at the end of the word have the stress before the suffix, e.g. _potential, understandable, futuristic, convenient, exemplify, information, ambitious, quantity_

When preparing for a presentation, make sure you know where the stress is in the important words you will use.

Exercise 7

You can find out which syllable is stressed in a word by looking in a dictionary. Look at the entries from the Collins COBUILD Advanced Dictionary for two words *developing* and *revenue*.

1   How many syllables are there in each word? How is this shown in the dictionary?

2   Which syllable is stressed in each word? How is this shown in the dictionary?

---

de|vel|op|ing /dɪv<u>e</u>ləpɪŋ/ ADJ [ADJ n]
If you talk about **developing** countries or the **developing** world, you mean the countries or the parts of the world that are poor and have few industries. ❏ *In the developing world cigarette consumption is increasing.*

rev|enue /<u>re</u>vɪnjuː/ N-UNCOUNT
revenue is money that a company, organization, or government receives from people. [BUSINESS] ❏ *...a boom year at the cinema, with record advertising revenue and the highest ticket sales since 1980.*

Not all dictionaries show word stress in the same way. Check the first pages of your dictionary for an explanation of how stress is shown.

Most online dictionaries show the pronunciation of a word in the same way as the entries you looked at in Exercise 7. Most also give a sound recording, so you can listen to the pronunciation.

Search for the word *developing* in the Collins COBUILD Advanced Dictionary website (www.mycobuild.com). Then click on the 🔊 icon to listen to a recording of the pronunciation.

Stress is also important in sentences. In Chapter 2, you learned about underlining key words in a seminar paper to help you stress them appropriately when speaking aloud. By using the correct stress, you will make your message clearer.

So, which words are the key words? People generally stress words that carry new information. Grammar words are not normally stressed, unless they are especially important. You will see more examples of this later in this chapter.

Exercise 8

Read and listen to the following sentences. Notice which words have stressed syllables. Look at the second sentence. Why do you think the words 'members' and 'council' are not as strongly stressed as other words? Think about the introduction of new information.

There are <u>15 members</u> in the <u>UN Security Council</u>. There are <u>five permanent</u> members and they <u>all</u> have to <u>agree</u> or the Council <u>can't make</u> a <u>decision</u>.

Exercise 9

Listen to the following sentences and underline the stressed words.

1   Let's look now at web browsers. I'm going to talk about three browsers – Opera, Safari and Firefox.

2   An eclipse is basically when a planet or star becomes invisible. A solar eclipse is when the moon passes between the Sun and the Earth.

3   We'll see two main kinds of language variation: geographic variation, and social variation.

When practising your presentation, make sure you stress the important words, those that give your audience new information.

Tip ✓ One very common reason to stress a particular word is to show contrast.

E.g.: *The country doesn't need to invest more in its <u>road</u> network. It needs to invest more in its <u>train</u> network.*

Improving fluency

Glossary

spontaneous
Spontaneous acts are not planned or arranged, but are done because someone suddenly wants to do them.

repeatedly
If you do something repeatedly, you do it many times.

The more your practise, the more fluent your presentation will become. Therefore, the best way to improve your performance is to practise your presentation aloud as often as possible and to speak English as much as possible. However, in this section you will see three particular areas of pronunciation that you can also work on to improve your performance:

- weak forms,

- joining words together,

- dealing with consonant clusters.

Since you will probably be speaking from notes, rather than from a script, you will not be able to include everything you look at here, as your speech needs to sound natural and spontaneous. However, when you practise, try out some of the pronunciation features explained in this chapter. As you apply them, they will feel more natural and it will be easier to use them in spontaneous speech.

You can also use what you study here to improve your pronunciation of any long words or phrases you know you will have to use in your presentation, for example, the word *implementation* or the phrase *distributed computing*. If you need to use certain phrases repeatedly, you can use some of the ideas here to help you make them sound as natural and fluent as possible.

It is important to remember that the pronunciation features outlined here should make things easier for you, not more difficult. If you find anything makes your performance worse, then concentrate on other areas.

Weak forms

You have learned how to stress key words containing new information in a sentence. So what happens to the other words which are not stressed?

Exercise 10

17

Read and listen to the following sentence. The stressed words are underlined. What do you notice about the pronunciation of the words in the boxes?

There are three areas to think about.

When people speak, they stress the 'content' words containing new information – like nouns, adjectives, adverbs and verbs. By comparison, many grammar words such as conjunctions, pronouns, etc. have a weak pronunciation. This is because they do not normally contain the key information in our message.

Exercise 11

18

Read and listen to the following sentences. The stressed words are underlined. Each sentence has one boxed word. You will hear two possible pronunciations after each sentence, a) and b). Tick the pronunciation that matches the boxed word in the sentence.

1   The map shows the main towns and cities in the area.   a ☐ b ☐
2   I want to look now at the negative consequences.   a ☐ b ☐
3   The policies were very effective.   a ☐ b ☐
4   We can look at this again at the end.   a ☐ b ☐
5   'Lula' da Silva was president of Brazil from 2003 to 2010.   a ☐ b ☐

All the words you saw in Exercise 11 were grammar words. They were: *and*, a conjunction (sentence 1); *I*, a pronoun (sentence 2); *were*, an auxiliary verb (sentence 3); *can*, a modal verb (sentence 4); and *of*, a preposition (sentence 5).

Generally grammar words like these have a weak pronunciation. The exception is if they are very important in a sentence. This often happens with negative verbs and when you want to emphasize something.

For example:

- *We <u>can't</u> be sure of the reasons for this.* (negative verb)

- *So I want to talk about all these things … <u>and</u> … try to explain why they happened.* (to emphasize the additional thing)

- *The government needs to work <u>with</u> local organizations, not <u>against</u> them.* (to emphasize the contrast between the prepositions)

Joining words together

In this section, you will read about how people join words together in natural speech. If you find certain word combinations or phrases difficult to pronounce, these techniques might be useful.

When we say a sentence, we do not say each word separately, with a clear gap between each. Read and listen to the following sentence.

I'm going to <u>talk about</u> a <u>number of issues and ideas</u>.

Notice that the final consonant of the underlined words joins onto the following word. So *talk about* becomes *talkabout* and *number of issues and ideas* becomes *numberofissuesandideas*. This is natural and correct – words that finish with a consonant generally join onto the following word if it starts with a vowel. In fact, you probably do this already when you speak in English, although perhaps not consistently.

But what happens when a word ends with a vowel? If the next word begins with a consonant, the two words often join together. Read and listen to the following sentence.

<u>My presentation</u> is divided <u>into three parts</u>.

Look at the underlined words. When they are spoken, they are joined together. Again, you probably sometimes do this naturally when you speak English.

Exercise 12

21

What happens when a word ending in a vowel is followed by a word beginning in a vowel? Listen to these three sentences. Which sound links the underlined phrases in each sentence? Match the sentences, 1–3, to the sounds, a–c.

1 The <u>media are</u> very powerful.	**a** /w/ (like 'win')
2 <u>We only</u> want to talk about one specific aspect of this.	**b** /r/ /(like 'run')
3 There are <u>two other</u> important points.	**c** /j/ (like 'yes')

We use the sound /w/ to link words ending with /uː/ (e.g. *new*, *few*) or /əʊ/ (e.g. *know*, *below*) to words beginning with a vowel.

We use /r/ with words ending /ɪə/ (e.g. *idea*, *fear*), /aː/ (e.g. *car*, *far*) and /ɔː/ (e.g. *law*, *more*).

We use /j/ with words ending /iː/ (e.g. *three*, *she*), /eɪ/ (e.g. *pay*, *way*), /ɔɪ/ (e.g. *employ*, *destroy*), /aɪ/ (e.g. *try*, *why*) or /i/ (e.g. *likely*, *forty*)

Note that in some varieties of English. For example, in US English, the final /r/ in word like *fear*, *car*, *far* and *more* is always pronounced.

Dealing with consonant clusters

Many non-native speakers find it difficult to pronounce some 'consonant clusters' – these are two or more consonants together in a word or phrase. In their speech, native speakers do not always pronounce all the consonants. Sometimes not including a consonant is considered incorrect, but there are many occasions where it is more natural not to include it. You can hear examples of this in the speech of politicians or journalists, such as in news broadcasts.

Exercise 13

Read and listen to the following sentences. Which sounds in the underlined words are not pronounced?

22

1   We <u>asked them</u> to complete the questionnaire within a week.

2   We <u>can't be</u> sure of the exact number.

3   Genghis Khan <u>lived between</u> 1155 and 1227.

4   The <u>next part</u> of my presentation will explain why.

5   I <u>haven't got</u> a library card.

6   This is the <u>last day</u> of my course.

The most common consonants to disappear in a cluster are /t/ and /d/. They often disappear in the middle of a consonant cluster, between two other consonants. For example in Exercise 13, sentence 2, the /t/ in 'can't be' disappears because it is between the consonants /n/ and /b/. The /k/ sound can also disappear when it appears between two other consonants, as in 'asked' in Exercise 13, sentence 1.

As you read before, it is not necessary to try to do this throughout your presentation; however, you might find it helps you to pronounce word combinations and phrases that have been causing you problems.

Remember

✓   Learn to control your breathing.

✓   Find out the right volume at which to speak at.

✓   Make sure you speak at an appropriate pace.

✓   Use intonation to help make your message clear.

✓   Find out where to put the stress on individual words.

✓   Think about which words need to be stressed in a sentence.

✓   Improve your pronunciation of word combinations and phrases by using weak forms and joining words together appropriately.

6 | Body language and eye contact

Aims
- ✓ appear relaxed
- ✓ choose between sitting and standing
- ✓ practise posture, position and movement
- ✓ think about where to look
- ✓ use your hands

❓ Quiz
Self-evaluation

Read the statements, then circle the word which is true for you.

1	I understand whether I should sit or stand when giving a presentation.	agree | disagree | not sure
2	I know how to stand correctly when I give a presentation.	agree | disagree | not sure
3	I know where to stand and when to move around.	agree | disagree | not sure
4	I know where to look when I am speaking.	agree | disagree | not sure
5	I know how to use my hands to support my message.	agree | disagree | not sure

The importance of body language

Glossary

observe
If you observe a person or thing, you watch them carefully, especially in order to learn something about them.

In this chapter, you will learn about three kinds of body language that are relevant when you are giving a presentation:

- where and how you stand,

- where you look,

- what you do with your hands.

However, the audience watches a speaker from the moment he or she enters the room, stands up or comes to the front to give a presentation. So think about what to do with your body from the moment you start and remember that people are observing you.

Exercise 1

Imagine this simple scene. You are at home, sitting on a chair or a sofa. Then you get up, walk across the room to pick up a book and return to your seat. Think about:

- how you would feel

- how you would walk

- how fast you would move

Glossary

casual
If you are casual, you are, or you pretend to be, relaxed and not very concerned about what is happening or what you are doing.

What you described in your answers is probably very different to how an inexperienced presenter feels and moves when getting up and moving to the front of the room to give a presentation. If you are inexperienced, you may feel worried about the audience watching you and this may affect how you move. You may walk faster than normal, you may take smaller steps and your shoulders might feel tense. If you have to put something down or pick it up, you might do it too quickly, so that it slips out of your hand or you drop it.

Look again at your answer to Exercise 1. What you described is approximately how you should try to move when you get up to give a presentation. You can try to look relaxed and comfortable even if you do not feel it. Remember, though, that, it is important not to appear uninterested or too casual.

By making an effort to move slowly and calmly, you will appear comfortable and relaxed to the audience. Acting calm and confident may help you feel it.

For more information on dealing with nerves, see Chapter 10.

Choosing between sitting and standing

One of the first decisions you will need to make about your presentation is whether to sit or stand. This will depend on the type of presentation you are giving, the size of your audience and the room where you are presenting. If you have any special needs that mean you need to sit, then speak to your lecturer privately.

Presenting

Exercise 2

Consider the following situations. Would it be better to stand or sit when giving a presentation in these settings?

1 Giving a seminar paper in a small room.

2 Giving a presentation that will be part of your score for a module, using visual aids.

3 Reporting on your progress with an ongoing research project.

Learning about good posture

Glossary

posture
Your posture is the position in which you stand or sit.

stiff
Something that is stiff is firm or does not bend easily.

If you choose to stand, it is important to be aware of your posture. Your posture affects how you appear to the audience and it can also affect your voice. You can improve your posture by:

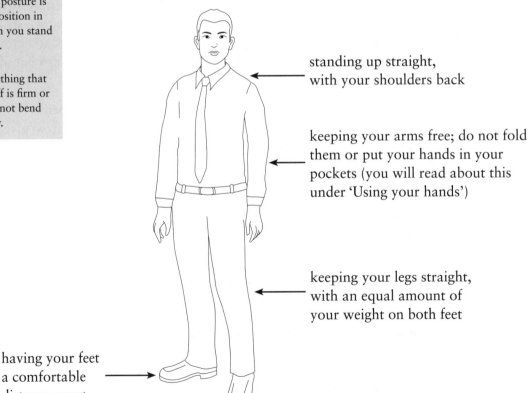

standing up straight, with your shoulders back

keeping your arms free; do not fold them or put your hands in your pockets (you will read about this under 'Using your hands')

keeping your legs straight, with an equal amount of your weight on both feet

having your feet a comfortable distance apart

Make sure that your body is not too tense or stiff. Keep your shoulders relaxed; your legs and knees should be relaxed enough so you can move easily. Standing like this, you will look and feel confident. You may also notice that good posture makes your voice clearer and louder.

Tip ✓ It is difficult to imagine what you look like standing. The best way to practise your posture is to look at yourself in front of a mirror, preferably a tall mirror where you can see your whole body. Practise speaking aloud, possibly using notes. Practise for a few minutes every week before your presentation. This will help you develop confidence in your posture.

Finding the right 'home position'

Glossary

layout
The layout of a garden, building, or piece of writing is the way in which the parts of it are arranged.

If you plan to give your presentation standing, it is important to decide *where* you will stand. While you may need to move around while speaking for different reasons, you should have a 'home position' that you return to.

Your home position is the place where you stand for most of your presentation. It should be a convenient and easy place to move from if you need to move around. It should also be a place that means you and your audience should be able to see each other well.

Your choice of home position will depend on the layout of the room and whether you need access to equipment, such as a computer or a projector screen, but you should think about the following things when choosing your home position:

- make sure all the members of your audience will be able to see you easily,

- make sure you are close enough to anything you need to use during your presentation, for example, a computer,

- make sure you do not stand in front of any visual aids.

Try to look at the room where you will give your presentation before the day that you give it, so you can decide on a suitable home position in advance.

Exercise 3

Look at the following illustrations showing different possible locations for presentations. Mark with an X where you think the best home position is in each illustration. Can you identify any problems in the layout of the rooms?

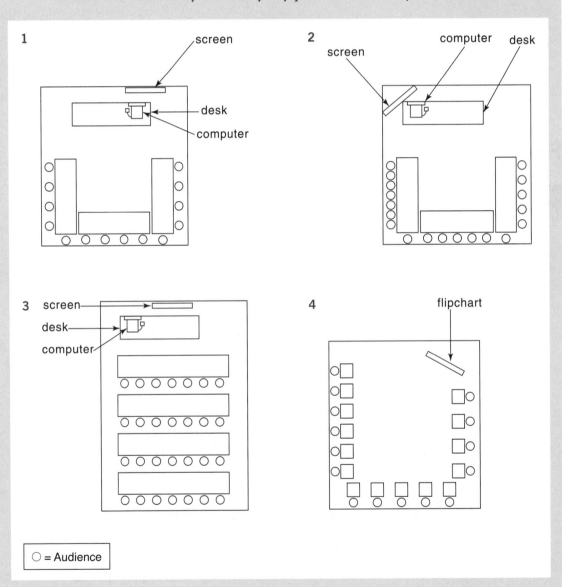

Moving

Glossary

still
If you stay still, you stay in the same position and do not move.

When you speak you will naturally want to move around a little. You will not look relaxed and confident if you stand completely still, like a statue, and moving around is often a good way of releasing tension and nerves. For example, when making an important point, you can move slightly towards the audience. You can also move to the left or the right as you look around the room at everyone. You can use your hands to support your points. (You will look at how to use your hands later in this chapter.)

While moving a little is good, it is possible to move too much. In fact, people often move a lot when they are anxious. Some common things nervous presenters do are:

- moving constantly from foot to foot,

- twisting their body from side to side,

- changing position frequently.

If you move around too much during your presentation, it can be distracting. Try to be aware of your movement and limit how much you move your feet. Practise in front of a mirror or with friends and notice what you do with your body while you are speaking. The more aware you are of your movements you normally make, the easier it will be on the day of the presentation to notice if you are moving too much.

There are a number of other reasons why you would move, during your presentation including:

- moving to your computer or to the overhead project to manage your visual aids,

- giving handouts to the audience,

- picking up an object from a table to show it to the audience.

If you have chosen your home position carefully, none of these actions should cause a problem.

For more information on using visual aids and handouts, see Chapters 8 and 9.

Visual aids and body language

You will look at how to create and use visual aids in detail later. Here you will look at how to use body language when using visual aids.

Exercise 4

Look at the following illustrations. Look carefully at the position of the presenter. Identify a problem in each situation. How could the presenter improve their positioning?

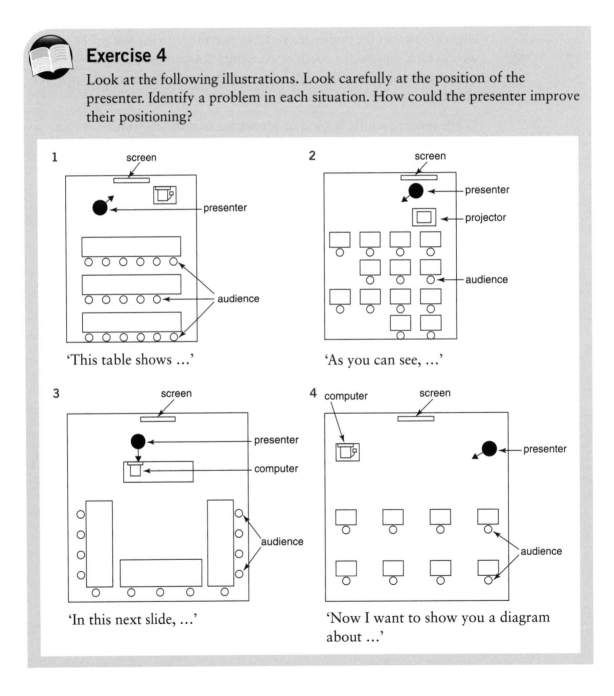

1 'This table shows ...'

2 'As you can see, ...'

3 'In this next slide, ...'

4 'Now I want to show you a diagram about ...'

You saw in Exercise 4 how important it is to plan where you stand, particularly when using visual aids. Remember to:

- keep your body turned slightly towards the audience, even when you are talking about or pointing at a visual aid,

- stand so that the audience has a good view of your visual aid, consider using a pointing stick or laser pen, or set up your PowerPoint slides to highlight what you want to show,

- stand away from visual obstructions, like computers, so the audience can see you clearly,

- ask someone to help you with your visual aids (e.g. changing slides), if possible.

For good examples of how to stand and move when using a visual aid, watch weather forecasts (you can find examples on www.weather.com or www.bbc.co.uk/weather). Notice how the presenters continue to face the camera while pointing to different parts of the map.

For more information on PowerPoint software, see Chapter 9

Gaze

Glossary
gaze Your gaze is the direction in which you look with your eyes.

Your gaze is an important feature of giving a presentation. It is crucial that you make eye contact with your audience while talking. When you make eye contact, the audience feels involved.

It can be difficult to remember to make eye contact. If you are speaking from notes, you may forget to look up at your audience from time to time, especially if you are worried about forgetting what to say.

Exercise 5

Practise making eye contact. Find a short text, such as a paragraph from this book. If you are preparing your presentation and have some notes ready, use one of your prompt cards. Then stand in front of a mirror with your text and read it aloud or give a part of your presentation. Concentrate on looking up at the mirror about once every five seconds, making eye contact with yourself. Do not worry if you make mistakes with what you say. Instead, focus on developing the habit of looking up regularly. When you are comfortable with this, look up more frequently, every four seconds and then once every three seconds.

With practise, you will find it natural to look up while you are speaking. You will be able to make eye contact frequently, without it reducing your ability to speak accurately and fluently.

Now, think more about exactly how to make eye contact with an audience. When you speak:

- move your gaze around the audience, looking at a different person each time,

- do not look at one person for more than a few seconds,

- make your gaze random and unpredictable (avoid looking at people in the same pattern, for example, at the left, then the middle, then the right, or at the front, then the middle, then the back),

- if you are presenting to a very large audience and cannot see people's faces, focus your gaze on areas of the audience rather than individuals.

Making real eye contact can feel embarrassing or uncomfortable. One way to manage this is to avoid looking people directly in the eye, but by looking at their forehead or nose. If you do this with people who are very near to you, they may notice. However, in a larger audience, people will not see the difference.

As the speaker, you may look around the room making eye contact and find that people in the audience have a blank expression on their faces. This is normal; it shows they are listening and concentrating on what you are saying. If you make eye contact with a person, you might find that they nod or smile. This does not necessarily mean that they are especially interested in your presentation. It is more likely that the person is being polite or feels embarrassed by the eye contact. Do not let this distract you. Move your gaze to the next person and make eye contact with them.

Tip ✓ When you are using a visual aid, look at it from time to time while speaking about it. However, always keep your body turned slightly towards the audience. Speak in the direction of your audience, rather than towards your visual aid.

Using your hands

Glossary

gesture
A gesture is a movement that you make with a part of your body, especially your hands, to express emotion or information.

metaphorical
You use the word metaphorical to indicate that you are not using words, images, or actions with their ordinary meaning, but are describing something by means of an image or symbol.

Your hands can be a very useful tool for your presentation. You can use them to support your communication and to make your presentation more interesting.

In 'Finding the right home position', you learned about choosing a home position. The same applies to your hands – when you practise, decide on a home position for your hands. Choose a position that is comfortable. If you are using one hand to hold your notes, decide what to do with the other hand when you are not using it. You could leave it by the side of your body or perhaps hold it behind your back. Avoid putting it in your pocket, as this looks too casual. Remember your home position and return to it after you have used your hand or hands for anything else.

If you use your hands incorrectly, their movement can be distracting. Avoid the following mistakes, which people often make when they are anxious:

- using too many gestures, which can be distracting,

- playing with things you are holding, for example, your notes or pens,

- touching your face, neck, hair or ears,

- placing your hand near or over your mouth, which blocks the sound and makes it hard to understand you,

- pointing at people, which can look aggressive. If you want to point at the audience (e.g. when asking them a question), point using your whole hand instead of a finger.

So when should you use your hands? Gestures can be very useful in making your message clear and involving your audience. It is possible to distinguish between different types of gestures:

- using your hands to make shapes that that are similar to real things (e.g. making a round shape when talking about a ball),

- using your hands to represent metaphorical meanings (e.g. moving a hand up to indicate an increase in a number),

- pointing to a visual aid or a specific part of a visual aid,

- 'beating' with one hand (moving or flapping it) to emphasize a particularly important point.

Presenting

Exercise 6

The gestures below are all examples of metaphorical gestures. Match the gestures 1–9 with different quotations from presentations, a–i.

1

   a   'And so that's the kind of thing we need to think about.'

2

   b   'In my opinion, …'

3

   c   'In the future, …'

4

   d   'Now, I want to bring all these ideas together.'

5

   e   'On the one hand, …'

6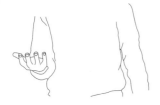

f   'So it's important to consider both of these factors before making a decision.'

7

g   'So what are some solutions to this problem?'

8

h   'We need to think of this as a kind of economic system.'

9

i   'And this has a really specific function.'

Exercise 7

Match the gestures, 1–9, from Exercise 6 with their meanings, a–i.

a   asking a question

b   combining different points or information

c   considering two different points at the same time

d   indicating one of two points of view

e   indicating precision

f   indicating the future

g   representing a chunk of text as an object

h   representing an abstract thing as an object

i   showing that something is a personal view

Many metaphorical gestures have different meanings in different languages and cultures. In English, for example, to represent the future, people gesture in front of themselves and for the past, they gesture behind. The gestures indicating past and future are not the same in all languages.

Tip   ✓   You may wish to check with a native English speaker if they understand all the metaphorical gestures you plan to use in your presentation.

Choosing to not engage your audience

In this chapter, you have learned how to use body language effectively in presentations, how to engage the audience and how to support the message that you are trying to communicate. However, there may be times during your presentation when you would rather *not* engage your audience. This could include:

■   when you are giving them time to look at a visual aid before talking about it,

■   if you have given a handout and they are looking at it,

■   during a pause, between sections.

In situations like these, there is no particular reason to engage the audience. In fact, if you continue to face your audience and make eye contact with them, they will expect you to continue talking. So it is advisable then to look somewhere else, for example, at a visual aid, if that is what the audience are looking at. Place your hands in the home position. You do not need to turn your body towards the audience. You can also move away from your home position.

When you move back to your home position, turn towards the audience and make eye contact again, it will be a clear signal that you are ready to start talking again.

Remember

✓ Try to move in a slow, relaxed way, even before you start your presentation.

✓ Decide whether to sit or stand when giving your presentation, based on the type of presentation, type of room and size of audience.

✓ Think about your posture.

✓ Decide on your home position, where you will stand for most of your presentation, so your audience has a good view and you are able to move easily.

✓ When using visual aids, keep your body slightly facing the audience and avoid talking in the direction of the visual aid.

✓ Make eye contact with the audience to involve them in your presentation.

✓ Decide on a home position for your hands and avoid distracting your audience with unnecessary hand movements.

✓ Use gestures to support your message.

✓ Turn your body away from the audience and avoid eye contact when you are not speaking and are creating a pause.

7 | Engaging your audience

Aims
- ✓ use inclusive language
- ✓ use simple language
- ✓ ask your audience questions
- ✓ learn to emphasize
- ✓ show your opinion

Aims

? Quiz
Self-evaluation

Read the statements, then circle the word which is true for you.

1	I understand what kind of language to use to make my audience feel more included in the presentation.	agree | disagree | not sure
2	I know the difference between formal, written language and spoken language, and which style is more appropriate for a presentation.	agree | disagree | not sure
3	I know how to use questions to make my presentation more interesting.	agree | disagree | not sure
4	I can use different techniques to emphasize important parts of my presentation.	agree | disagree | not sure
5	I can share my opinion in different ways, appropriate to the setting.	agree | disagree | not sure

What you have learned so far

In this chapter, you will learn about the different techniques and language styles you can use to engage your audience as much as possible. It is important to make your audience feel involved, as this will make the presentation more interesting for them. However, as academic presentations are quite formal occasions, your presentation should be similar to the lectures and presentations you see at university – you need to hold the attention of the audience, in a way that is appropriate to an academic setting. You have learned about many ways of doing this in this book so far. Exercise 1 gives you a quick review of what you have already learned.

Exercise 1

Match the sentence beginnings, 1–10, with suitable endings, a–j. Create sentences showing advice you have already learned in the book.

1 If you have to read a written text,	**a** and a clear conclusion that summarizes what you said.
2 Consider your audience when deciding on your content,	**b** so you can be seen easily by your audience and you do not block any visual aids.
3 Have a clear introduction that prepares your audience for what is going to come,	**c** so your audience knows where you are in your presentation and where you are going.
4 Give an interesting fact in your introduction	**d** by thinking about what they already know and what you want them to learn.
5 Use 'signposting' phrases at different stages of your presentation	**e** to get your audience's attention at the beginning.
6 If you speak from notes instead of reading from a script,	**f** because the way you say things helps make your message clear.
7 Use intonation and stress effectively	**g** the audience will feel involved in the presentation.
8 Choose an appropriate 'home position' to stand in when presenting	**h** your speech will be more natural and easier to follow.
9 Use hand gestures	**i** to support your message visually.
10 If you make eye contact with your audience,	**j** underline the key words to stress and mark the pauses so that it is easier for your audience to follow.

In the rest of this chapter, you will learn new techniques you can use to make your presentation effective. You will learn more about how to involve and engage the audience better.

Using inclusive language

One of the simplest techniques you can use to engage your audience is to be aware of the pronouns you use when speaking.

Exercise 2

Read the following pairs of sentences. Which sentence in each pair do you think would be more engaging for your audience?

1 a This graph shows the decrease in road deaths.
   b We can see the decrease in road deaths in this graph.

2 a I think you can all see how important this data about farming is.
   b I think this data about farming is important.

3 a This helps us to understand why a public transport system developed.
   b This explains why a public transport system developed.

The pronouns 'you', 'we' and 'us' and the phrases 'you all', 'we all' and 'us all' are inclusive and help to engage your audience.

Using simple language

Glossary

terminology
The terminology of a subject is the set of special words and expressions used in connection with it.

You have already looked at how spoken language is different from written language. To review this, look back at Chapter 4.

In your presentation, you will probably need to use specialized terminology, which is likely to be formal. Because academic presentations usually take place in quite formal situations, it is usually inappropriate to use very informal language in them. However, when you do research for your presentation, you will read formal, written texts, such as books and journal articles with formal terminology. Remember that the kind of vocabulary you see in these texts is not always appropriate for a spoken presentation. Avoid using very formal words in your presentation when you can think of a more appropriate, spoken alternative. This makes your presentation more accessible to the whole audience. Remember not everyone in the audience will know as much as you do about the topic and using specialist terminology may make it difficult for some people to understand what you are saying.

Compare the two sentences.

> **Formal, written:**
> *There is <u>much</u> discussion on how effective the process is.*
>
> **Less formal, spoken:**
> *There is <u>a lot of</u> discussion on how effective the process is.*

The first sentence is not wrong. However, the word 'much' is quite formal when used in an affirmative sentence. While this sentence would be appropriate in a formal, written context, the second sentence sounds more natural in spoken language.

 Exercise 3

Replace the underlined words in sentences 1–8, with the more informal words in the box.

a lot of	go back	happen	look at	main	quite	show	work out

1   The <u>principal</u> reason for the increase is well known.

2   Let's <u>return</u> to the topic of treating ear infections.

3   The medical staff were able to <u>ascertain</u> the cause of the baby's illness.

4   It's <u>somewhat</u> difficult to be sure of the reason.

5   When you add water, some interesting results <u>occur</u>.

6   <u>Much</u> research has been carried out on water purification techniques.

7   If you <u>examine</u> modern crime data, some common trends emerge.

8   All these things <u>demonstrate</u> why we need to find a solution.

If you use appropriate spoken language, instead of the words usually found in formal, written texts, the audience will find your presentation easier to follow and more engaging.

Questions

Another simple, effective technique you can use is asking questions. It is not advisable to ask 'real', direct questions during a presentation, because generally, the audience is expecting only to listen. However, you can ask your audience questions that you do not expect them to answer. This type of question is called a 'rhetorical question'.

Exercise 4

Read these three examples from presentations. Match the examples, 1–3, with the techniques, a–c.

1 'So, what are the main factors that can cause inefficiency in the design of cars? Well, firstly let's talk about 'drag'.'	a asking a rhetorical question, which requires no answer
2 'But we've already seen that this conclusion isn't valid, haven't we?'	b asking a series of questions together, which you will answer later
3 'What was the initial cause of the financial crisis? Was it the mortgage crisis in the USA? Or did it start much earlier, with government financial policies?'	c asking a question and answering it immediately

As you saw in Exercise 4, you can use different types of questions to involve your audience. The effect is the same – although nobody will answer the questions, your audience should feel more involved and engaged.

One of the reasons why people ask questions in presentations is because it helps make the presentation sound more conversational. Asking a question leaves the audience wanting to know more about the topic and then by answering it, you can guide your audience to your point of view.

Be careful not to ask too many questions though as it may become boring and the audience will stop listening.

Exercise 5

Look at the pairs of example questions, 1–6. Match the correct function a–f, to each pair.

a   to give more details about something

b   to say how to solve a problem

c   to say the reason why something happened

d   to say what happened next

e   to talk about the function of something

f   to talk about results

1   So, what was the cause?
    So, why did this happen? } _____

2   So, what can be done?
    So, what's the solution? } _____

3   So, what happened then?
    So, what followed this? } _____

4   So, what does this mean?
    So, what is this exactly? } _____

5   So, what is the result of this?
    So, what is the effect of this? } _____

6   So, what does this do?
    So, what's the function of this? } _____

Tip ✓ It is much better to use short questions than long questions because long questions are harder to process. Compare these two questions.

What were the results of our survey of 100 current Economics students in the US university system? ✗

*We surveyed 100 current Economics students in the US university system. **What were the results?*** ✓

81

Emphasizing

There will be many occasions in your presentation to emphasize information that is especially important. In Chapter 5, you learned about using stress to emphasize certain words.

Exercise 6

Listen to the following sentence. Notice how the word *can* is stressed.

23

We can't be sure why the empire fell, but we *can* make some good guesses.

In positive sentences, it is not normal to stress auxiliary verbs (*do*, *have*, *be*) and modal verbs (including *can*, *may*, *will* and *should*). However, they can be stressed to emphasize them in a sentence.

Exercise 7

Now listen to the following sentence. Notice how the word *not* is stressed.

24

That's *not* what we're going to analyse today.

The word *not* is not normally stressed, but it can be stressed for emphasis.

Exercise 8

Listen to the sentences and underline the auxiliary or modal verb that is stressed.

25

1   We do need to think about some other factors.

2   This has happened before in other tests.

3   The antivirus software should detect it, but it doesn't.

4   This result did surprise us, as it was the opposite of what we expected.

5   It doesn't matter now, but I think it will be important in future.

Tip ✓   If a sentence is in the present simple or past simple and does not already contain an auxiliary or modal verb, add *do*, *does* or *did* to add emphasis. Look again at Exercise 8, sentences 1 and 4:

*We **do** need to think about some other factors.*
*This result **did** surprise us, as it was the opposite of what we expected.*

Structures for emphasis

You can also use some grammatical structures to emphasize important parts of a sentence. Look at Exercise 9 to see some examples of this.

Exercise 9

Read the sentences. Underline the part of each sentence which is emphasized.

1   What I want to talk about today is tardigrades, which are tiny animals also known as 'water bears'.

2   What you need to do is to write what you think the answer is in the box.

3   What we need to think about is where the waste will be stored.

4   What we should remember is that the participants in the study might not be representative.

Different parts of each sentence were emphasized in the examples you saw in Exercise 9.

1   To emphasize a **verb and an object** in a sentence, use this structure.

What + subject + verb + *to do* + *be* + *(to)* + infinitive ...

> **For example:**
>
> *What you need to do is to <u>write what you think the answer is in the box</u>.*

2   To emphasize an **object,** a *that* **clause,** or **a** *wh-* **clause,** use this structure.

What + subject + verb + *be* + | object.
| *that* clause.
| *wh-* clause.

> **For example:**
>
> *What I want to talk about today is <u>tardigrades</u>.*
>
> *What we should remember is <u>that the participants in the study might not be representative</u>.*
>
> *What we need to think about is <u>where the waste will be stored</u>.*

Glossary

anticipation
Anticipation is a feeling of excitement about something pleasant or exciting that you know is going to happen.

These structures (sometimes called 'fronting' or 'cleft sentences') are very useful in presentations, as they create a feeling of anticipation in your audience. When the first part of the sentence tells them something is coming, they are interested to hear the rest of the sentence. The structures also make your message easier to understand: if you divide the sentence into two parts, it is easier for the audience to process the two parts separately.

Exercise 10

Rewrite the following sentences, using the *What* structures, to emphasize the parts that are underlined.

1   You're going to see <u>a summary of the results</u> now.

   What _____.

2   We should think about <u>how to improve on the research methods</u>.

   What _____.

3   They thought <u>that the website design would increase profits</u>.

   What _____.

4   I'd like you <u>to keep this image in your head</u> while I speak.

   What _____.

5   We then looked at <u>where the biggest technological innovations seem to be happening</u>.

   What _____.

6   We need <u>to look at some of these results in more depth</u>.

   What _____.

7   I showed you earlier <u>a photo of the nuclear reactor</u>.

   What _____.

8   We hope <u>that we'll have some more definite results next year</u>.

   What _____.

Another technique which can be used to emphasize a part of a sentence is to start a sentence with *it*. These sentences are normally used to contrast a piece of information with something else already mentioned. Look at these examples.

- All these factors are important, but <u>it's the price of energy that</u> has the biggest effect. (emphasizing the subject: *'the price of energy* has the biggest effect')

- That brings us to the topic of climate change, and <u>it's this that</u> we're going to look at next. (emphasizing the object: 'we're going to look at *this* next')

- Scientists researched radioactivity for decades, but <u>it was in 1938 that</u> they discovered nuclear fission. (emphasizing a time phrase: 'they discovered nuclear fission *in 1938*')

- The industrial revolution affected most parts of the world, but <u>it was in Britain that</u> we really saw the first signs. (emphasizing a place: 'we really saw the first signs *in Britain*')

These sentences all use this structure:

It + be + emphasized phrase *+ that …*

Exercise 11

Rewrite the phrases in brackets using the *it* structure to complete the following sentences. Emphasize the underlined part of the phrase.

1   There are lots of important consequences of GM foods, but I think

_____ (the <u>environment impact</u> is the most significant).

2   _____ (The country needs <u>investment</u>), not loans.

3   The phrase 'united nations' was first used officially in 1942, but

_____ (the organization was created <u>in 1945</u>).

4   The United Nations has offices in Geneva, Nairobi, and Vienna, but

_____ (the General Assembly is held <u>in New York</u>).

Showing your stance

In addition to your explanation of factual information, in your presentation you should normally show your personal stance. Presentations are more engaging if they are not entirely factual and descriptive. Depending on your brief, you may have to do a substantial amount of original research for your presentation or you might need to give some basic, descriptive information. Whatever your brief, think about whether you would like to add a personal angle, in an appropriate way.

Look at the following sentences. The underlined words are adverbs. Notice how they add a personal angle to the facts.

- <u>Obviously</u>, we need to do some more research to investigate this hypothesis.

- <u>Interestingly</u>, not all writers agree on the best way to define 'translation'.

You can use adverbs at the beginning of a sentence to show your opinion and make a presentation more engaging.

 ## Exercise 12

Match the adverbs, 1–6, to their meanings, a–f.

1 apparently	**a** basically
2 essentially	**b** I would like … to happen
3 fortunately	**c** it is very logical that …
4 hopefully	**d** it was not expected that …
5 presumably	**e** luckily
6 surprisingly	**f** it seems to me that …

Tip ✓ Adverbs and adverbial phrases are useful. You can use them at the start of a sentence to show other meanings, in addition to sharing an opinion. You can use *furthermore* and *additionally* to add another point, *overall* to introduce a summary, *consequently* to show a result, *actually* to correct or contradict something and *generally* to say that something is true most of the time.

You can also indicate your stance by adding a comment clause to the end of a sentence, using *which*.

> **For example:**
>
> *The President appoints judges in the Supreme Court, <u>which is important for a lot of reasons. First,</u> ....*
>
> *None of the respondents reported having more than ten hours of free time a week, <u>which was quite surprising</u>.*
>
> *There are now probably more non-native speakers of English than native speakers, <u>which is incredible, when you think of it</u>.*

When you add a comment clause like this, you always use *which*. The clause usually refers back to the whole of the sentence.

Remember

✓ Use inclusive language to make your presentation more engaging.

✓ Use natural, spoken language, so your presentation sounds natural.

✓ Ask questions to involve your audience.

✓ Use different techniques to emphasize important parts of your presentation.

✓ Show your stance by using adverbs and relative clauses.

8 | How to use visual aids

Aims ✓ learn about different types of visual aid

✓ make visual aids that are useful and effective

✓ learn language to refer to visual aids

✓ think about practical considerations when preparing visual aids

✓ deal with problems with visual aids during your presentation

 Quiz
Self-evaluation

Read the statements, then circle the word which is true for you.

1	I know about different types of visual aid and when to use them.	agree | disagree | not sure
2	I understand how to create useful and effective visual aids.	agree | disagree | not sure
3	I know words and phrases to use when referring to visual aids.	agree | disagree | not sure
4	I know about practical things to think about if I plan to use a visual aid.	agree | disagree | not sure
5	I know about the kinds of problems that can occur when using visual aids and how to overcome them.	agree | disagree | not sure

The advantages of using visual aids

Glossary

cognitive psychologist
A cognitive psychologist studies how people think, remember, speak, and perceive.

Cognitive psychologists have observed two main things about how people learn.

- Our brains process information that comes in through our eyes (visual information) and our ears (verbal information) separately.

- Our brains can only pay attention to a few pieces of visual information and a few pieces of verbal information at a time.

Exercise 1

Think about what you have just read about how people learn. How can visual aids help your audience to follow your presentation?

However, it is still not completely clear how people learn. Some studies have shown that when the visual information and the verbal information given in a presentation are the same – in other words, when the things that a speaker says are also presented visually *as written text* – that this can actually make it *more* difficult to process the information. So this means that it is probably better to speak and use *images* than to speak and use *text*.

Visual aids can certainly help you to make a presentation easier to follow. In addition to this, your lecturers will probably expect you to produce and use visual aids for a formal presentation. However, it is important that you choose your visual aids with care, paying special attention to how you use written text. This chapter will help you do this.

First, look at some of at the different types of visual aid you may be able to use when you give your presentation.

Types of visual aid

The most common types of visual aid used at English-medium universities are:

- blackboards and whiteboards (including interactive whiteboards),

- flipcharts,

- overhead projectors (OHPs),

- PowerPoint presentations,

- handouts,

- video recordings.

Exercise 2

Write the names of the visual aids under the correct illustration.

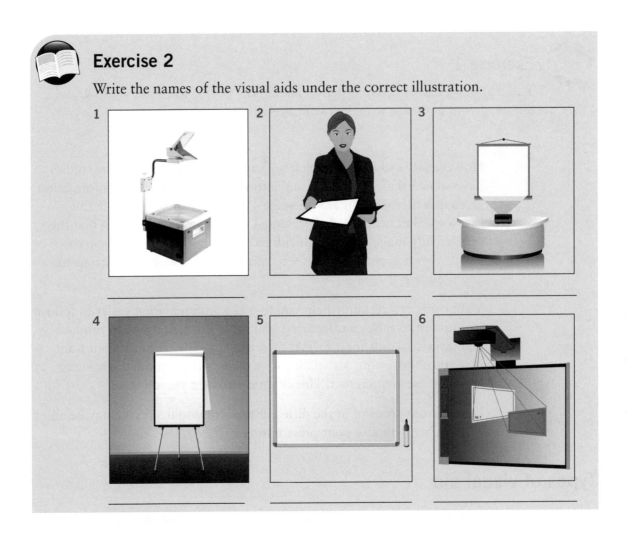

Advantages and disadvantages

Most lecture halls and seminar rooms will have a blackboard or whiteboard. Using a blackboard or whiteboard can be a good way to support what you are saying. However, as writing on the board means you turn your back to the audience and is quite time-consuming, it is not very suitable in a formal situation. If you are making a formal presentation and you do not prepare a PowerPoint slideshow, but simply write on the board, it may also look like you are not well prepared.

In addition to a blackboard or whiteboard, the room might have a **flipchart** that you can work with. If you have access to flipchart paper, you can prepare your visual aid in advance, so you avoid some of the disadvantages of whiteboards. One disadvantage is that flipcharts are quite small, so harder to see and you cannot fit very much information on them.

convenience
If something is done for your convenience, it is done in a way that is useful or suitable for you.

sophisticated
If something is sophisticated, it is advanced or complex.

Overhead projectors (OHPs) are becoming less common, as many universities now have the technology for students to show PowerPoint presentations. When using an OHP, you need to use *transparencies* – transparent plastic sheets that you print or photocopy on in advance or write on during the presentation. If you write on the transparencies during the presentation, this can make it more interactive. Many people consider OHPs rather old-fashioned now and students usually prefer the convenience of PowerPoint slides over preparing transparencies.

PowerPoint presentations are probably the most common tool used by students when giving presentations. With PowerPoint software, you can include text, audio and video to create a sophisticated presentation. The main disadvantage is that people may overuse the power of the software.

For more information on PowerPoint presentations, see Chapter 9.

Handouts are sheets of paper, often photocopied, given to the audience. They are something to keep and are a good way of giving more detailed information. You can make your handouts interactive by including gaps for the audience to complete while they are listening. One disadvantage is that a handout can take the focus off you, the speaker. You might notice people reading through the handout instead of listening to you speaking.

Your presentation may include a **video recording**. In the past, videos or, more recently DVDs, were used. Today, people usually play any audio or video via a computer and projector, perhaps as part of a PowerPoint presentation.

Exercise 3

Which of the visual aids you have read about:

1   might be unsuitable for formal presentations?

2   rely on computers?

3   allow you to create sophisticated designs?

4   give the audience something to keep?

5   might be hard to see in a bigger room?

6   can be prepared in advance?

Exercise 4

Which visual aid would you choose for each of these situations? There may be more than one possible answer.

1   You have to give a five-minute presentation in a seminar about a chapter of a book.

2   You have to give a short presentation about a research project you are working on.

3   You have done some group work during a seminar or lecture and you have to talk about what you discussed.

4   You have to give a formal presentation as part of the assessment for a module.

Tip   ✓   Always make sure you know in advance what equipment will be available to you for your presentation.

What visual aids can contain

You can use visual aids for different reasons. Often a presenter will use a visual aid at the beginning and at the end, to summarize basic information related to the presentation. For example, at the beginning, it is common to include:

- an introductory slide with the speaker's name and the title of the presentation,

- an outline of the presentation.

And at the end, it is common to include:

- a summary of the presentation,

- references for any sources used.

See 'Example introductory and conclusion slides' on pages 119–120 for examples of these kinds of slides.

Tip   ✓   Anything you include in a visual aid which is taken from another source (e.g. a quotation or a diagram, chart or map from a book) needs to be cited correctly. For help with this, see appendix 3 – Citations and references on page 162 or the student handbook from your university.

Visual aids can also be useful in the main part of your presentation. You are most likely to use some or all of the following:

- text,

- images (photos, illustrations, diagrams and tables),

- audio recordings,

- video clips.

We can make a distinction between two types of visual aid. The main purpose of using visual aids is to support the information you are presenting orally. However, depending on your topic, visual aids can be useful if you need to talk about something visual, for example, a graph, a work of art, a table, logo or a product design.

Supporting your message

How you choose to use visual aids that support what you are saying is very important. Here are some research findings:

- it is easier to follow spoken words rather than words written on a visual aid during a presentation,

- it is easier to follow a presentation if it contains words and relevant images rather than only words,

- it is easier to follow a presentation if no unnecessary or irrelevant information is included in visual aids.

Exercise 5

Think about what you just have read. Read the following statements and decide if they are true or false.

1   It is advisable to limit the number of words in a visual aid.

2   Images may look attractive, but they do not make your presentation easier to process.

3   It is advisable to remove anything from a visual aid that is not totally relevant to the presentation.

4   It is better to communicate more complex information by putting text in a visual aid than by trying to explain it verbally.

Exercise 6

Look at the following examples of visual aids, 1–4. What problems can you identify with them? How could they be improved?

1

> Anita Roddick:
> 'The term "globalisation" has come to mean something very specific, but the idea of an inter-connected world – linked by appreciation of each other's cultures and the ability to see injustice in the formerly darkest corners of the world – has a great deal of resonance for people like me … It may be that the IT revolution makes this possi-ble, but – according to Jerry Mander – we still have to be very vigilant.'

Source: Roddick, Anita. 2001. *Take it Personally*. London: HarperCollins, p. 27

2

Wang Ting

High-speed rail: USA

- top speed = 180–240 km/h
- high-speed rail more attractive:
  - ☐ fuel prices
  - ☐ airport security
  - ☐ environment

Bachelor's Degree in Transport Management

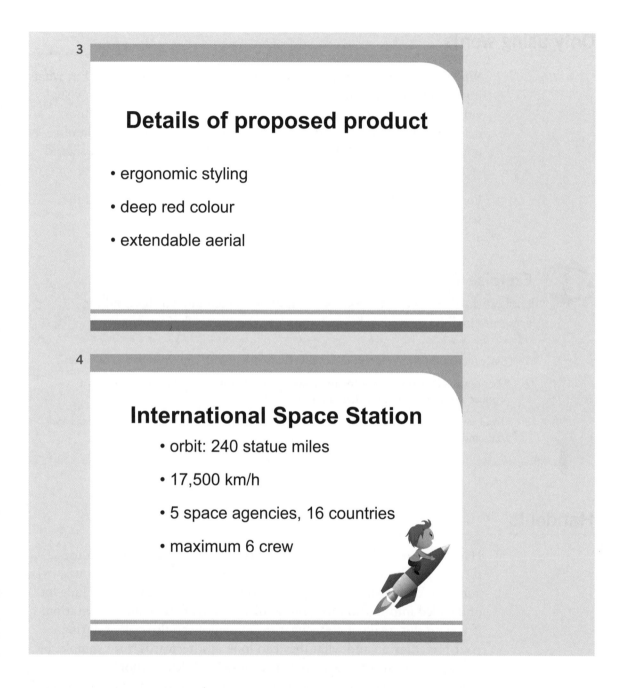

The choice of image to use in a visual aid will depend on the topic you are presenting. It is important that the image is appropriate to the context. Avoid using cartoons, as they are not normally suitable in an academic presentation. Think instead about the type of visuals you find in your textbooks or the handouts you receive from lecturers at your university.

Only using words

When you use an image, it should support what you are saying. But what if you cannot find a suitable image? In this case, you can create a visual aid with key words to reinforce what you are saying. You will almost definitely use these key words when you are speaking, but you should not simply read aloud the text on your visual aid. The visual aid should support your words, not the other way round.

For advice on how to choose the key words for a visual aid, read the section on making notes in Chapter 4.

Exercise 7

Look at the three excerpts from presentations. Which keywords could the presenter include on a visual aid to support what he or she is saying?

1   'Since the 1970s, many recessions have been associated with large increases in oil prices.'

2   'User-centred design means software designers should think about the end-users of a product at every stage of the design process.'

3   'Top-level managers, like Chief Executive Officers (CEOs) and presidents, create plans and goals and make decisions for a whole company.'

Handouts

Handouts are a bit different to other types of visual aid. You can use them as an alternative to OHPs and PowerPoint slides, to give your audience key words and images. However, handouts can also include lots of detailed information for your audience to read after the presentation. If you do this, make it clear what the audience should look at during your presentation and what they can look at afterwards, for example, by saying 'I don't want you to look at ... now' or 'Please ignore ... for the moment'. Alternatively, you can give out the handouts at the end of the presentation.

Handouts can also be useful for members of the audience who have problems with their vision and might not be able to see other visual aids very well.

Tip ✓ As soon as you display a visual aid, the audience will start looking at it and stop listening to you. Only display your visual aids when you want your audience to look at them and no longer listen to you.

Referring to visual aids

Glossary

explicitly
If you do something explicitly, you express or show it clearly and openly, without any attempt to hide anything.

When you are using a visual aid to support your spoken content (e.g. a slide containing key words), you do not normally need to refer to it explicitly. However, when you want to look at and analyse a visual aid in detail, prepare your audience by using some phrases to warn them you are about to start talking about it.

Exercise 8

Listen to presenters introducing and referring to some visual aids. Complete the following useful phrases.

26

Referring to visual aids

1 _____ you can _____ in this table, …

2 _____ graph _____ …

3 _____ you _____ _____ this slide, what _____ can _____ is …

4 _____ a _____ _____ this graph.

5 _____ we _____ _____ the next slide …

6 I'd _____ you to _____ _____ this table, which _____ …

Tip ✓ If you present something complicated in a visual aid, first give the audience a few seconds to look at it and process it. Then start talking about it.

It is also common to refer to the visual aids that you are going to use in a presentation and those that you have already used. This can help link different parts of your presentation together and helps prepare your audience for what is going to come later.

Exercise 9

Complete the following phrases, using the verbs in the box.

see	remember	come	explain	come	show

Talking about visual aids you have shown or will show.

1   We'll _____ to that in the next table.

2   We'll _____ some graphs about that later.

3   I'll _____ why in the next few graphs.

4   I'm going to _____ you some slides about …

5   _____ that quote right at the beginning …

6   We'll _____ back to this table later in the presentation.

Focusing on and explaining the message in a visual aid

Sometimes, when using visual aids, you will need to focus on one particular part or certain parts of them. This could be because you are showing a complex image and you want to concentrate on just one part of it.

For example, if you are showing your audience a table with different numbers, you might want to talk about one or two of the numbers after looking at the whole table. Or if you are showing a graph, you might want your audience to focus on different parts of it that are particularly important.

Note, however, that it is better to try to avoid showing very complicated visual aids. Try to simplify visuals like tables and graphs as much as possible so that only the most important information is included and your audience is not distracted by irrelevant information.

Exercise 10

Read and listen to part of a presentation. Notice the underlined phrases that the presenter uses to help the audience to focus on particular parts of the graph.

27

OK, so have a look at this chart. It shows the percentage of the population staying on in education after the age of 16, in 2000 and 2010. <u>If you just look at</u> the left part of the chart, you can see that the number of young people staying on beyond 16 has increased in that ten-year period. But <u>take a closer look</u> at the centre part. You can see that the number staying on beyond 17 was the same in 2000 and 2010. Now <u>focus on</u> the part on the right – here we can see that the number staying on past 18 has actually fallen.

Exercise 11

Now read and listen to the presenter continuing.

28

What this shows us is that while there are fewer people leaving school at 16, there are also fewer people staying in education at 18, meaning fewer people going on to study for higher-level qualifications.

Notice here that the speaker explains the messages in the visual aid to the audience. This is not necessary with every visual aid, but it can be very helpful to explain visuals with numerical information, such as a table or a graph. For information on language you can use to talk about numbers and figures, see 'Talking about numbers and figures' on page 157.

Exercise 12

The presenter you listened to used the phrase 'What this shows us is …' to introduce the message. Put the following words in order to make similar phrases.

1 that message the is here _____

2 this looking say can that we at _____

3 because this important is _____

4 is that what this highlights _____

Exercise 13

1   Imagine you have to describe the graph below in a presentation. Describe the table and record yourself doing this, if possible. If you cannot record yourself, write a description. Remember to:

- introduce the table,
- talk about some particular parts of the table,
- explain the message of the slide.

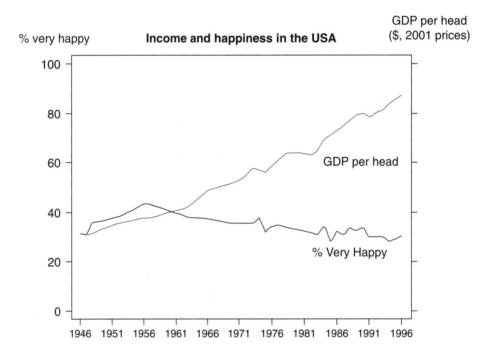

Note: GDP means 'Gross Domestic Product', the total value of all the goods and services that a country produces in a year.

Source: Layard, R. (2003) Happiness: has social science got a clue? Lionel Robbins Memorial Lectures 2002/03

 2   Now listen to the audio track and compare your text or recording with it.

Practical considerations

Whatever kind of visual aid you decide to use, it is important to consider the practical factors when you are planning. In general, it is advisable to practise a day before the presentation, if possible in the room where you will give your presentation. Find out from your lecturer if you can access the room. If so, you can test your presentation and make sure all the technology works. If not, perhaps you can arrive an hour early on the day and do all your checks then.

Before the day of the presentation, think about the following.

- If you are using a blackboard, do you have chalk and a cloth to clean the board?

- If you are using a whiteboard, do you have the right kind of marker pens ('dry wipe', not permanent ink) and do they have plenty of ink in them? Are you going to use pens with colours that can be easily seen from a distance? Be particularly careful with red ink, as it can be hard to read from distance – stick to blue and black as much as possible.

- If you are using a flipchart, can you position it so everyone can see it? Is it big enough that when you write, people at the back of the room can read it? Do you have the correct pens for writing visibly? (Try to find ones specifically for flipcharts, as whiteboard markers are not suitable for writing on paper.)

- If you are using OHP transparencies, do you know how to use the projector? Do you know how to adjust the size of the image? And the focus?

- If you are using PowerPoint software, does your presentation look the same when you open it on the computer you are going to use (which may have a different version of the software)? Look out in particular for the positioning of text, as sometimes the layout of PowerPoint slides changes when you open the files on a different computer.

- If you are giving handouts, find out how many people will be in the audience at your presentation so you know how many copies to make. It is advisable to make a few more, in case more people attend than you expect.

Exercise 14

Read the following advice from some presenters. Decide which visual aids or aids each piece of advice refers to. There may be more than one visual aid related to each piece of advice.

1   'Make sure you number your transparencies. It's easy to drop them or mix them up in a presentation and if they are numbered, it will be much easier to reorganize them.'

2   'Ask someone to stand at the back of the room and see if they can see everything easily. If not, think about what changes you need to make.'

3   'Make sure you can log in to the computer you want to use. Keep a copy of your file on a memory stick and email yourself a copy, just in case there are problems.'

4   'It's a good idea to have a "neutral" slide to put on when you need to – it could be blank or just a very simple image. This way you can make sure everyone is listening to you, instead of looking at your visual aid.'

5   'Remember the lights. Ask someone to be responsible for turning down or off the lights, so your visual aid is more visible.'

6   'To get an idea of how clear your slides are, print them out on paper and put them on the floor. Then stand and look down at them. If they're not clear to you now, they probably won't be clear to the audience when you show them on the screen.'

When things go wrong

If you prepare in advance and check things as much as possible, you should not have any problems during your presentation. However, as things can still go wrong, it is worth planning how to manage the situation if you do experience a problem.

Exercise 15

1   Listen to three people commenting on a presentation. Which of the three visual aids does each speaker have a problem with?

30

| video | OHP slide | PowerPoint slide |

2   Listen again. Which speaker deals with the problem well? What mistakes do the other speakers make?

It is always a good idea to have a printed copy of any visual aid you are planning to use. You can use the print-out to help you summarize anything if you have any practical problems. You should also be very familiar with your visual aids, so you can talk about them confidently.

Remember

✓ Think about what kind of visual aid is appropriate for the type of presentation you will give.

✓ Think about what equipment is available and try to access it before you do your presentation, to practise and make sure everything works.

✓ Use visual aids to support what you want to say.

✓ Keep text on visual aids to a minimum and make sure that you include nothing irrelevant.

✓ Use appropriate language when referring to your visual aids.

✓ Consider the practical details of using visual aids when planning your presentation.

✓ Make sure you know what to do if you have a problem with a visual aid during your presentation.

9 | Tips on using PowerPoint software

Aims
- ✓ find alternatives to PowerPoint software
- ✓ identify common mistakes
- ✓ add content
- ✓ master basic formatting and design
- ✓ carry out final checks

Aims

? Quiz
Self-evaluation

Read the statements, then circle the word which is true for you.

1	I know of other software packages that can be used instead of PowerPoint software.	agree | disagree | not sure
2	I know some common problems with PowerPoint presentations.	agree | disagree | not sure
3	I know how to add content on PowerPoint slides.	agree | disagree | not sure
4	I understand how to format and design PowerPoint slides.	agree | disagree | not sure
5	I can select appropriate images to use in an academic presentation.	agree | disagree | not sure
6	I know how to focus on particular parts of a slide using PowerPoint software.	agree | disagree | not sure
7	I know what things to check before giving my presentation.	agree | disagree | not sure

PowerPoint software and alternatives

PowerPoint software allows you to create slides on a computer, which can be very useful for when you are giving a presentation. This software is part of the Microsoft Office™ package and is probably installed on the computers at your university.

There are other types of presentation software, some of which are free. While the advice in this chapter mainly relates to PowerPoint software, as it is the most commonly used presentation software, much of what this chapter covers can also be applied to other software.

If you do not have access to PowerPoint software, there are many free alternatives. Here are the two most common alternatives.

- OpenOffice.org™ (found at www.openoffice.org), a free alternative to Microsoft Office™, contains a free piece of presentation software called Impress. Versions are available for Windows and for Apple Mac. If you use Impress, you can save your files in the same format that PowerPoint software uses, so you can use them on a computer with either Microsoft Office™ or OpenOffice.org™.

- Google Docs (found at Google Drive: drive.google.com) is an entirely online office package. It contains a presentations programme which (like OpenOffice.org™) allows you to save your presentation in the same format as PowerPoint software.

Exercise 1

1 Check your own computer and the computers at your university. Do you have PowerPoint software? Do the computers at your university have it?

2 Check which version of PowerPoint software the computers have. Normally, you can do this by clicking on 'Help' and then 'About PowerPoint'. A newer version of the software can usually open files from an older version, but the opposite might not be true. So make sure you can open your presentation on all the computers you will use.

3 If you do not have access to PowerPoint software, you can download OpenOffice.org™ or create an account on Google Docs. Test their presentation software to learn how it works.

What does presentation software do?

Presentation software, helps you to create visual aids to use in a presentation. Its basic function is to show text and images on screen, although it can also play video or audio recordings.

PowerPoint software is based on the concept of 'slides' – each slide appears as a full screen when you 'play' the presentation. You can move from slide to slide using the mouse or the keyboard, or you can set your presentation so that the changes are automatic. For each slide, you can choose different features, such as colours, styles and backgrounds. You will learn about using these features in this chapter.

Common mistakes with presentation software

Because presentation software is extremely powerful, preparing slides to show during a presentation can be a very effective technique for presenting information and supporting communication. However, there has been a lot of criticism of how presentation software is sometimes used.

One of the main disadvantages of presentation software is that it offers so many choices that it is easy to misuse. For example, it is easy to add colour, visual effects, animations and images and the result of this is that people sometimes create presentations that are so complex that they distract the audience from the message that they are trying to communicate. While your lecturer will probably expect you to produce and use attractive visual aids, remember that the most important thing is what you say and how you say it.

In Chapter 8, you learned about some of the practical problems related to using visual aids. You learned that it is advisable to limit the number of words on a visual aid and to avoid irrelevant information or images. This advice also applies to presentation software. However, there are also many other mistakes that people make when using presentation software. Do Exercise 2 to see some of these errors and read some advice on how to avoid them.

Exercise 2

Read the advice on using presentation software, 1–8, and match it with the correct explanation, a–h.

1 'Be careful about using "Clip Art" images – the cartoons and illustrations included with software.'	**a** If you make a small image bigger, it can become unclear and difficult to see, especially when it is projected on a big screen.
2 'If you use an image, be careful when you enlarge it.'	**b** Make sure they are pleasant to look at and easy to read, including on a big screen.
3 'Think very carefully about the colours you use.'	**c** They are often too informal for an academic presentation and can make your presentation look unprofessional.
4 'If you want to show something from the internet, don't rely on the internet working in the room where you're presenting.'	**d** Anything that is not relevant to what you are saying can distract the audience from your message.
5 'Don't structure your spoken presentation around your PowerPoint presentation.'	**e** You might have a problem with the internet connection on the day of your presentation, so it is better to download what you want to show and save it on your computer or in your presentation.
6 'Avoid putting everything you want to say on your slides.'	**f** You should use the software to support what you want to say, not to organize it.
7 'Make sure you don't include anything on your slides that isn't relevant to what you say, including the university name and logo, the title of the presentation, and so on.'	**g** You will probably get more marks for the content of what you say and how you say it, than for how attractive your PowerPoint presentation looks.
8 'Prioritize your research and your preparation of the spoken part of your presentation, rather than your PowerPoint presentation.'	**h** Your audience want to hear you speak, not read your slides. What you show on the screen should only support what you say.

Do not worry if some of the terminology in this exercise is unclear. You will learn it as you work through this chapter.

The content of your PowerPoint presentation

Before you start creating your presentation slides, make sure that you have done all or most of your research and planned your spoken presentation well. Remember that your slides should not contain everything that you are going to say. Rather, they should *support* your content. First prepare your spoken presentation and then plan your slides. When you have finished planning what you are going to say, you can work out how to support it by using your slides.

Adding content

When you create a new presentation with PowerPoint software, the first slide is automatically formatted as a title slide. This means that there is space at the top for a big title and space underneath for a subtitle.

After this, any new slides added will have space at the top for a title and a space below for some text, organized in bullet points. Your slide title should be short and simple and should make the audience curious. For example, in a slide discussing the key features of a product, you could make the heading a question, such as 'What makes this product unique?' instead of 'Key features'.

You can use the space in the slide with the bullet points for key words to support what you are saying.

A slide can also contain visual material, such as photos, maps, tables, graphs and charts, and also video and audio recordings. In PowerPoint software, you can usually insert material by using the 'Insert' menu. It is also possible to use the clip art that comes with the software or can be downloaded from the Microsoft website (office.microsoft.com).

For more information about choosing key words, see Chapter 4.

Tip ✓ There will be times when you do not need any visual aids to support what you are saying. Leaving a previous slide on the screen can be distracting to the audience. You should therefore create a blank slide with a black background to show when you need no visual support. Change to this slide when you want the audience to listen to you and look at you.

Bullet points

As mentioned previously, PowerPoint software automatically creates bullet points for you to organize your text. However, presentations with bullet point lists are often criticized. In Exercise 3, you will find out why.

 Exercise 3

Read some criticisms about bullet point lists in presentations. Complete the gaps with the following phrases.

in order of importance	what you are saying	complex information	lots of text

1   'Bullet points may encourage you to write _____. No matter how much you type, PowerPoint software automatically resizes the text so that it fits on the screen.

2   Bullet points may make it look like the list is _____, with the most important things at the top and the least important at the bottom, even if this is not what you mean.

3   Bullet points may make you oversimplify _____, so it fits easily into a list.

4   Bullet points give people something to read, when they should be listening to _____.

So how can you avoid these problems related to bullet points? The first thing to know is that bullet points can be very useful and effective, when used correctly. Furthermore, many university lecturers use them in presentations and expect students to do the same, as it is probably the most common way to format slides.

The most important thing is to think about how to use bullet points well. Avoid having too many bullet points on one slide; use no more than three or four. Avoid making the text for each bullet point too long; keep to three or four words per point.

Tips ✓   Unless all the bullet points in a slide are relevant at the same time, you should make each bullet point appear one by one. To do this, use the 'Appear' function found in 'Animations' in PowerPoint software. By applying 'Appear', you can reveal each bullet point to your audience only when it is relevant.

✓   You may discover that your presentation software offers many other animation effects for changing how the text appears. Many of these effects are inappropriate for an academic presentation, as they can be distracting. For a university presentation, it is advisable to use only the 'Appear' effect.

Alternatives to bullet points

Instead of using bullet points, you can present your text more creatively. You can offer less information, but make your audience think more. Look at the following two slides, one using bullet points and the other with the text displayed differently.

U.N. General Assembly: voting

- one member, one vote
- majority votes = win
- in some situations: two thirds
  majority needed

U.N. General Assembly

Who votes?

How do you win?

Slide with bullets · Slide without bullets

Another alternative to text is to use a powerful image to support your message. On a slide, you can have just an image and a title, or a combination of an image, title and a very small amount of text. Take care when choosing an image, as selecting the right one can be difficult.

Choosing and using images carefully

Including images can be an excellent technique to support your presentation. Depending on which software you are using, there may be a good selection of photographs, as well as illustrations, that you can use in your slides. Photographs are often more effective than images, especially now the quality of projectors has improved and photographs can be shown very clearly.

You saw in Chapter 8 that one way to use images is to support the information you are presenting orally. It is possible to use quite abstract images to do this.

Exercise 4

Match the following images, 1–4, to the topics the speakers will cover in their presentations, a–d.

a   Identifying the most important data

b   Energy needs in the developed world

c   Public transport needs in the next five years

d   Making links with institutions abroad

1

2

3

4

Source: Shutterstock

However, it is very easy to use images inappropriately. For example, many people use the clip art that is included with PowerPoint software. However, think carefully about whether all these images are appropriate and relevant to your presentation. Just because an image is available in PowerPoint software that does not mean it will be right for a presentation. Including cartoons, in particular, can look unprofessional and might not have a positive effect on your audience.

Whenever you are choosing an image for your presentation, remember one important thing: only choose an image if you are sure that it supports what you want to say and that it also makes your message clearer to your audience. Never choose one just because it is attractive.

Exercise 5

Look at the following images, which all come from PowerPoint Clip Art. Which of them do you think would be suitable for an academic presentation?

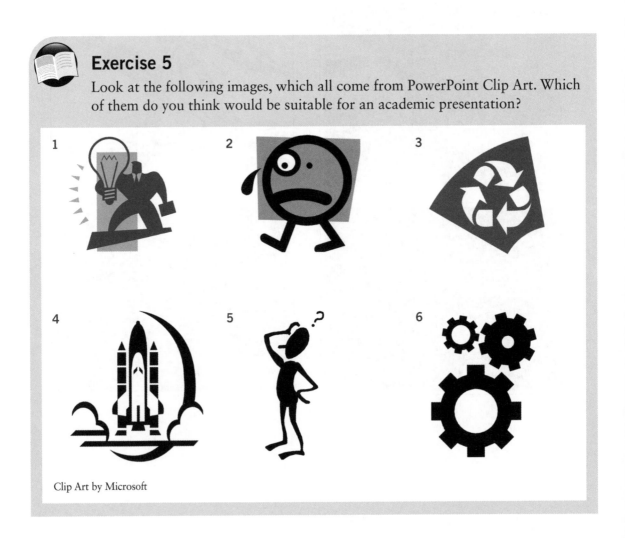

Clip Art by Microsoft

Glossary

drag
To drag a computer image means to use the mouse to move the position of the image on the screen, or to change its size or shape.

ratio
A ratio is a relationship between two things when it is expressed in numbers or amounts. For example, if there are ten boys and thirty girls in a room, the ratio of boys to girls is 1:3, or one to three.

crop
If you crop a photograph or image, you cut off part of it.

In addition to the photos included in PowerPoint software and those that you can download from the Microsoft website, many other websites offer free, high-quality photographs that you can. You can find them by searching for free stock photos and copyright-free images. These websites include:

- www.compfight.com

- www.morguefile.com

- www.sxc.hu

- commons.wikimedia.org

Most of the images you can find from the sites listed above are available for you to use for free in an educational context as long as you acknowledge where you found them. You should be able to find specific details about this listed for each image.

Smaller images appear distorted when you enlarge them, especially when you project them onto a big screen. For your work, choose large, high-quality image files. If you want to resize an image, drag it at the corner not at one of the sides – this will keep the height-to-width ratio the same and avoid changing the shape.

You can also crop an image to remove unwanted parts of it or if you want to make it a particular shape or size so it can fit more easily on a slide.

Tips
✓ If you make an image fill up a whole slide, it can be more attractive and effective than displaying it in a smaller size, inside a slide. When an image fills up a slide, you can still include a title and some text. Choose colours for the text that contrast with the image, so it is easy to read.
✓ If you are having problems making the text on top of an image readable, right-click the text box and choose 'Format shape'. Then choose a fill colour and set the transparency to around 25–50 per cent.

Basic design settings

Glossary

font
In printing and graphics, a font is a set of characters with the same style and appearance in all its letters of the alphabet and numbers, e.g. Times New Roman.

consistent
If a book or document is consistent, it has a similar style or appearance throughout.

Presentation software gives you many options to change the appearance of your presentation. The basic features to think about are:

- font size and type,

- background,

- colours.

Try to make you presentation consistent, by using one style throughout. When a presentation has different fonts, backgrounds and colours in every slide, it is distracting and makes it difficult to follow the content. A consistent, appropriate style looks professional and is easier to understand.

Use large font sizes to keep your presentation easy to read. PowerPoint software automatically sets the text to a large size when you create a slide. Avoid making it any smaller. If you type a lot of text, the software will automatically make it smaller so it can fit on the screen, but you need to avoid having slides crowded with small text. Remember that although text may look big when you are creating a slide on your computer, it will appear very much smaller when it appears on the big screen.

Fonts

When choosing a font, you need to think about two important features: type and variety. First, choose a type of font that is appropriate in an academic presentation. Second, avoid using a large variety of different fonts, as this can be distracting. Use a maximum of two or three and be consistent with them, for example, use one font for all your titles and another for your bullet points.

In a presentation, it is advisable to use a 'sans serif' font, like Arial and Helvetica. Sans serif fonts look clean and can be read clearly, when there is a small amount of text. Avoid using a 'serif' font, however, like Times New Roman or Garamond. Serif fonts are more suitable for longer, dense text, like essays and reports.

> **For example:**
>
> Sans serif: Arial and Halvetica
> Serif: Times New Roman or Garamond

Exercise 6

Look at the pairs of phrases below. Which do you think is more appropriate for a slide in an academic presentation, a) or b)?

1	a	Summary of results	b	Summary of results
2	a	FOUR KEY IDEAS	b	four key ideas
3	a	Previous research findings	b	**Previous research findings**
4	a	**Spending in 2012**	b	Spending in 2012

Avoid writing in capital letters. If you want to emphasize a word it is better to use **bold** or to <u>underline</u> it.

Only use professional-looking fonts. For example, Comic Sans was designed, as its name indicates, to look like the font used in comic books and is inappropriate in academic presentations. Finally, avoid any fonts that may be unclear or difficult to read. Remember that it is more difficult to read text when it is projected on the screen than when you look at it on your computer screen.

Colour

Choose the colour for your font very carefully. The font should be easy to read and look professional and attractive when projected onto a big screen. It should never clash with your images or background. Remember to be consistent: you probably only need a maximum of two or three colours. You could choose two or three shades of a single colour (e.g. a lighter and a darker green); a range of colours that are fairly close together (e.g. blues and greens); or complementary colours (e.g. red and green or blue and orange).

Backgrounds

You will need to choose a background for your slides. You can choose a single colour, an image or a pattern.

It is advisable to choose a simple background, which will look clean and attractive when projected onto a screen. What you choose should not clash with any of your text or images. Although it is possible to choose a different background for each slide, it is better to have one main background for most of your presentation, even if you sometimes decide to show a full-screen image. This will make your presentation visually attractive and consistent.

PowerPoint software offers a number of 'themes' to choose from. These themes contain automatic settings for the background, colours, font size and the layout of a presentation. It is better to create a look for your presentation that matches what you want to communicate than to use one of these themes. However, if you decide to use a theme, choose one of the simpler ones and make sure it is appropriate for your presentation.

Transitions

Transitions are effects you can choose, for moving from one slide to the next. While PowerPoint software offers many different effects, think carefully about how appropriate they are for an academic presentation. Avoid selecting a transition that will be a distraction. Many people find the 'Fade' effect to be the simplest and most appropriate for academic situations. Choose one transition and use it consistently.

Exercise 7

Choose the correct option for each piece of advice, based on what you have learned.

1   Use a *small* / *large* variety of fonts.

2   Text often looks *smaller* / *bigger* on a projector screen than on your computer screen.

3   *Serif* / *Sans serif* fonts are usually clearer for slides.

4   Use a maximum of *two or three* / *five or six* different font colours.

5   Choose something *simple* / *complex* for the background of your slides.

6   Choose *one transition effect* / *two or three transition effects* to use in your presentation.

Creating focus

When you are speaking to the audience, you may wish to explain particular points on one slide. This could be a single word or phrase or part of a diagram or image. You can do this by pointing or using a laser pen, but you can also use a simple technique to 'create focus', i.e. highlight parts of a slide in an elegant and professional way.

To create focus, first make copies of the slide you will be discussing. On PowerPoint software, you can normally do this by right-clicking on the slide and selecting 'Duplicate Slide'. Leave the first copy of the slide as it is. You can show the full slide first, then focus on specific parts by proceeding to the next slides you have created.

Now change the appearance of the part or parts of the slide you *do not* want to focus on. Draw a rectangle (click 'Insert', then 'Shape') around the parts of the slide you *do not* want to focus on. Then right-click on the rectangles and set the transparency to 50 per cent, making sure that the rectangles have no borders, shadow effects, and so on.

Look at the following examples of a slide indicating the years in which certain countries joined the United Nations.

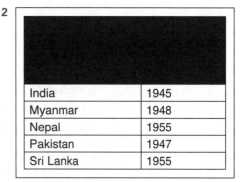

1

UN Member States	
Member	**Date joined**
Bangladesh	1974
Bhutan	1971
India	1945
Myanmar	1948
Nepal	1955
Pakistan	1947
Sri Lanka	1955

Original slide

2

India	1945
Myanmar	1948
Nepal	1955
Pakistan	1947
Sri Lanka	1955

Slide with first rectangle added

3

India	1945

Slide with both rectangles added

4

UN Member States	
Member	**Date joined**
Bangladesh	1974
Bhutan	1971
India	1945
Myanmar	1948
Nepal	1955
Pakistan	1947
Sri Lanka	1955

Slide with rectangles at 50% transparency

You can change the settings you use, perhaps by choosing different colours or different levels of transparency. To create a dramatic effect, you can leave the rectangles in black. By setting transparency at about 50 per cent, you create a more subtle effect. Obviously, it is possible to create a focus in many different parts of the slide. For each new focus, you just need to create another duplicate slide.

This technique can be applied to anything on a slide; images, text, graphs and tables. To create the focus you want during your presentation on a particular part of the slide, you simply need to move to the next slide you have created.

Final checks

As many things can go wrong with PowerPoint presentations, try to minimize the risk of these problems. At least a day before your presentation, work through this checklist:

- Run a spell check. Make sure you have set the language of the file to English (Click 'Tools', then 'Language') or this will not work properly.

- Print out all your slides. If you type notes below your PowerPoint slides, these will be printed too.

- If you are doing a group presentation, create one PowerPoint file containing all presentations, instead of each speaker having a separate file. Opening files or changing windows in the middle of a presentation looks unprofessional.

- Check that you can log in on the computer you will be using and that you can open your presentation on it.

- Once you have opened the presentation, check that all the slides appear as you have planned.

- If you are using your own laptop, check how to plug it into the projector and make sure it functions correctly.

Introduction and conclusion slides

You will need to think about your introduction and conclusion slides. These are important so make sure you spend some time on these slides. Here are some examples of layout and the kinds of points you should include.

Ilana Bodini

Cooperatives in rural communities in South East Asia

BSc Economics

The first introductory slide usually gives the speaker's name and presentation title.

Outline

- overview
- relationships with states
- case study
- future directions

The second introductory slide contains an outline of the presentation. Note that there is no logo in this slide.

Summary

- overview
- relationships with states
- case study
- future directions

The first conclusion slide is a summary of the presentation. Note how similar it is to the second introduction slide.

References

Trilly, R. (2011). Cooperation in South East Asia. In *Asian Economics Review* 15(4). pp. 142–155

Ferguson, T. (2008). Jakarta and Cooperatives: a case Study. In *Systems of Economic Journal* 3(1). pp. 44–51

The second conclusion slide gives the references. Remember that it is important to cite the sources you have used and to provide a reference list.

Remember

✓ If you do not have a copy of PowerPoint software, free alternatives are available.

✓ Use presentation software to support what you are saying, not to speak for you.

✓ Avoid using too many bullet points; use creative alternatives.

✓ Only use images that are appropriate for an academic presentation.

✓ Format your presentation so it looks professional and attractive and the text is easy to read.

✓ If you want to focus on particular slides, you can set them up with certain features, in advance.

✓ Check that everything will work as you planned, the day before your presentation.

10 | Preparing, rehearsing and dealing with nerves

Aims ✓ revise what, why, where and how to rehearse
        ✓ rehearse in groups
        ✓ deal with nerves
        ✓ overcome negative thoughts
        ✓ build confidence

Aims

Quiz
Self-evaluation

Read the statements, then circle the word which is true for you.

1	I know why it is important to do a full rehearsal.	agree	disagree	not sure
2	I understand what to concentrate on when practising.	agree	disagree	not sure
3	I know what factors to consider when practising for a group presentation.	agree	disagree	not sure
4	I can apply some techniques to control my nerves.	agree	disagree	not sure
5	I know some advantages of feeling nervous.	agree	disagree	not sure
6	I understand how to avoid negative thoughts and build my confidence.	agree	disagree	not sure

Finalizing your presentation

Glossary

rush
If you rush, you do something too quickly because you do not have much time.

In earlier chapters, you learned about researching, deciding on content, preparing notes and creating visual aids. In the days before your presentation, you will probably be very busy getting everything ready. However, make sure you do not leave too much preparation until the last minute. In student presentation sessions, where the audience are also the presenters, you will often see members of the audience making last-minute changes to their presentations or finalizing details, while other speakers are giving a presentation. This is not a good situation to be in, for several reasons.

Exercise 1

Imagine that while a speaker is giving their presentation, a fellow student is making last-minute changes to their PowerPoint slides or having a conversation. What kind of impression does the student's behaviour create? Think about:

- the lecturer
- the other speakers

Glossary

dedicate
If you dedicate time to something, you spend time doing it.

effective
Something that is effective works well and produces the results that were intended.

If you are making last-minute changes, in addition to creating a negative impression on the other presenters, students and your lecturer, there are certain other disadvantages. Firstly, you are more likely to make mistakes. If you are under time pressure and are rushing, you will have little time to check your work. While rushing, you may introduce new errors.

You will also miss the opportunity to watch the other presentations and to see your fellow presenters going through the same experience, which can calm your nerves. The presentations will give you something to concentrate on and you may worry less about yours. You will learn more about this later in this chapter, under 'Dealing with nerves'.

Try to finalize everything before you go into the presentation room, even if you know that you will have to wait for your turn to speak. If you are working in a group and have not finalized everything the day before, organize a group meeting for before you go into the room. You will learn about rehearsing in groups in this chapter.

The benefits of rehearsing

Glossary

rehearse
When people rehearse a presentation, play, dance, or piece of music, they practise it in order to prepare for a performance.

Now think about rehearsing. Many inexperienced presenters do not rehearse. Instead, they spend more time preparing their content or visual aids. However, if you dedicate some time to rehearsing, you will see a big improvement in your performance. There are several reasons why rehearsing presentations is effective.

Exercise 2

Complete the headings with the following words.

problems	technology	timing	whole	voice	automatic

1   Rehearsing makes your performance more _____.

When you give a presentation, you may have many things on your mind and a lot of input going into your brain (e.g. faces in the audience and noises). All this will take up some of your attention. The better rehearsed your presentation is, the more automatic it will be and the less these distractions will affect you.

2   Rehearsing helps you be sure about _____.

Many people find that when they start rehearsing, they realize they do not have enough time to fit in all the content they were planning to. You can never be certain about timing, until you do a realistic rehearsal.

3   Rehearsing helps you gain confidence with any _____ you plan to use.

If you do not have much experience of using PowerPoint presentation software or other types of visual aid, rehearsing will give you an opportunity to practise and become more familiar with it and make you more confident on the day of your presentation.

4   Rehearsing gives you a better idea of your presentation as a _____.

When you are preparing a presentation, you concentrate on many small details. Sometimes, until you do a rehearsal, it is difficult to see the 'big picture' – how all the parts of your presentation work together.

5   Rehearsing helps you identify _____.

When you go through the process of rehearsing a presentation, from start to finish, you sometimes find problems that you were not aware of before. For example, you might identify places where you need to change the order of your presentation. You may also identify mistakes in your visual aids.

6   Rehearsing gives you the chance to check you are using your _____ effectively.

If you rehearse with other people, you can check whether you are speaking loudly enough to be heard at the back of the room, whether you are speaking at a good pace and whether your pronunciation of key words and phrases is clear.

Remember that even the most experienced speakers rehearse their presentations. When you watch a very competent presenter, they may appear natural and spontaneous. This is probably because they have rehearsed and are confident with what they are presenting.

How and what to rehearse

You have covered some advice about rehearsing in earlier chapters of this book. Do Exercise 3 to see what you remember.

Exercise 3

Match the sentence halves, 1–5, with a–e to make full sentences. They will form sentences that revise some of the advice you have learned in this book.

1 Organize the time you have for preparing and practising your presentation carefully	a to develop your ability to look up and make eye contact with the audience.
2 If you are reading from a script, mark the stress on key words and pauses and record yourself reading it	b to make sure your performance sounds interesting and is easy to understand.
3 Practise speaking from your notes in front of a mirror	c that will support your message during your presentation.
4 Prepare and practise the pronunciation of key phrases you know you will use	d so you still have plenty of time to rehearse.
5 Prepare and practise gestures	e so you will manage them well during the presentation.

Final rehearsals

It is important to practise individual aspects of your presentation, and you should do this whenever you get the chance, perhaps at home in your bedroom. However, you should also do a final rehearsal of the whole presentation, in as realistic a setting as possible. Only by doing this will you get a real idea of what to expect on the day. Try to do a final rehearsal in the room you are presenting or in a very similar room.

Tip ✓ Find out where you will be giving your presentation. If it is in your normal seminar room or lecture hall, ask your lecturer if you can use the space before or after one of your normal sessions, to do a rehearsal.

Thinking about timing

In Chapter 5, you learned about pace. You learned that you should normally aim to talk at about 120 words per minute. However, until you do a full rehearsal, from start to finish, you cannot be sure of how long a presentation will last.

Even your rehearsal time might not be entirely accurate, however. So it is advisable to plan a presentation that is slightly shorter than your time limit. For example, if your brief is to do a 15-minute presentation, consider preparing only 10–12 minutes of material. This is because when you do the real presentation, many little delays will slow you down. You might pause while someone moves a chair or comes in late, you might interact more with the audience than you expected or you might need longer than planned to emphasize an important point.

All these delays can combine to make a presentation longer than expected.

Other things to concentrate on

There are many other things to consider when doing a final rehearsal. Exercise 4 will help you identify other factors to consider.

Exercise 4

Complete the sentences offering advice with the following words.

access	layout	lighting	position	space

1 Think about your _____ . Where's the best place to stand? You learned about 'home positions' in Chapter 6.

2 Think about _____ . If you have a laptop, is there room for it? Is there a power source free where you can plug it in? Is there space to put any handouts? Where will you put your bottle of water?

3 Think about _____ . Will you need to turn off the lights to make your visual aids clearer? Where are the light switches? Does a lot of sun come into the room? Are there any blinds you can close? Do you know how to open and close them?

4 Think about _____ to equipment. If you need to use the computer, will you be able to reach it from where you plan to stand? Will you need someone else to help you change slides?

5 Think about the _____ of the room. Is the position of all the chairs and tables suitable? If you are giving your presentation in a teaching room, it should already be set up correctly for presentations. If not, can you move the furniture around?

> **Tip** ✓ Many inexperienced presenters worry that they will finish too quickly and consequently prepare too much content for their presentations. However, it is rare for a presentation to take less time than expected. Avoid preparing too much or, on the day of your presentation, you may need to rush or to leave some parts out.

Rehearsing in groups

If you are working in a group, there are extra things to consider when you plan to rehearse. The first step is to arrange a time when the whole group can meet and rehearse together. Even if it is difficult to find a time when everyone is free, it is important to make an opportunity to rehearse your presentation together.

Now consider specific things that are relevant to rehearsing for a group presentation.

Exercise 5

Read the following advice about rehearsing for group presentations, 1–6. Decide which area, a–c, each one is related to.

a   when changing from one speaker to the next

b   when you are not speaking

c   when using visual aids

1   Make sure the appearance of all the different speakers' work is consistent. Not everything needs to be identical, but it does not look very professional if the design changes significantly when each new speaker starts.

2   Decide on a good place for everyone in the group to sit. They should be close to where you are going to speak, but not so close that they might be distracting.

3   Make sure that in every speaker's introduction of the next person, they introduce what the next person is going to say *accurately*.

4   If you are using presentation software, the rehearsal can be a good chance to combine all your files into one single file. Keep this 'master file' somewhere safe and make sure that if anyone makes any changes later to their visual aid that they make the changes on the master file, too.

5   Practise the way a speaker should walk up to the presentation area, and the route the next speaker plans to take. Make sure there is no chance the two speakers will bump into each other as one walks on and the other walks off.

6   Practise what the other speakers in the group should do before or after they have had their turn. They should pay attention and listen to the speaker instead of looking through their notes or talking to each other, for example.

Tip ✓ When you introduce the next speaker, move your gaze between the audience and the next speaker. You can use make a gesture with an open hand to draw the audience's attention to the new speaker.

Dealing with nerves

Glossary

diligent
Someone who is diligent works hard in a careful and thorough way.

In Chapter 1, you learned about the concerns many people have about giving presentations. You saw that many of your worries may disappear the more you prepare for a presentation. When you first receive the brief for your presentation, it may appear very difficult. However, after you have done your research, prepared and rehearsed, you will probably feel more confident and the task will seem less difficult to you.

On the day of your presentation, even if you are thoroughly prepared, you may still feel anxious. This is quite normal. Even very experienced speakers sometimes feel nervous. In this situation, remember that feeling nervous can actually help you. How? Think about the following points.

- Nerves can make you work harder. Being worried about giving a presentation can make you spend more time preparing and rehearsing for it.

- Nerves can make you more diligent. Being worried can make you check your work more thoroughly for errors.

- When you speak, being nervous can give you extra energy and help you give a good performance.

In the next few pages, you will learn about some techniques for dealing with nervous feelings. While nerves can be a problem, remember that these feelings do not have to be negative. They can help you too.

Exercise 6

How do you feel when you are nervous? Write a list of symptoms and sensations you experience. Think about what happens to different parts of your body, for example your hands or your heart.

When you wrote your answers to Exercise 6, you probably listed some of the following symptoms:

- starting to breath fast
- feeling like you cannot breathe properly
- feeling your heart is beating fast
- getting shaky hands
- feeling your legs become weak

- sweating
- feeling your mouth become dry
- feeling dizzy
- feeling tired
- getting a headache

It is important to understand that even if you experience some of these symptoms or sensations it does not mean you cannot give a presentation. Even if you feel very anxious, you can almost certainly still stand and speak. Your nervousness can be unpleasant, but it cannot stop you from doing what you need to.

Overcoming negative thoughts

If you are worried about your presentation, you may find that when you think about it, negative thoughts come into your head. For example, you might worry that you will forget what you have to say and how embarrassing that would be.

It is important to stop and identify these negative thoughts and try to analyse them. Ask yourself:

'How probable are the negative things I am imagining? How bad would the consequences really be?'

When you analyse negative thoughts like this, you will probably see that your fears are unlikely to become a reality and if they did, the consequences would not be so bad.

Then, every time a negative thought comes back, remember the analysis you did. By doing this, you will replace a negative thought with a positive, helpful one.

Exercise 7

Match the negative thoughts, 1–6, to the helpful thoughts, a–f, that you can use to replace them.

1 I have problems with pronunciation and nobody will understand me.

a If you rehearse and check the equipment, probably nothing will go wrong. If something does go wrong, however, you can still give your presentation verbally and communicate your message successfully.

2 My grammar isn't very good and I'm embarrassed about making mistakes.

b It is possible that the audience will have trouble understanding a few words. However, they will understand almost all of what you say, so this is not a serious problem.

3 There are more intelligent students in the audience who know much more than me about the topic I'm discussing.

c Nervousness shows much less than people think it does, so the audience might not even notice. Even if you show your nerves, most of your audience will sympathize. It will not affect what you are trying to communicate.

4 Everyone will see how nervous I am and think I'm stupid.

d It is not necessary to give an extremely interesting or entertaining presentation. The important thing is to communicate content to your audience. If you do this, they will be interested.

5 I want my presentation to be interesting and entertaining, but I think it will be really boring.

e You might make mistakes, but this is not very important. The important thing is that you communicate something to the audience. That will happen, even if you make mistakes.

6 I'm sure something is going to go wrong with my PowerPoint slides in the middle of the presentation.

f Your preparation will make you very knowledgeable about your topic. Even if some of the audience know more than you, they will still find your presentation interesting.

Exercise 8

Do you have other negative thoughts about your presentation? If so, write them on the left. On the right, write helpful thoughts to replace them.

Negative thought	Helpful thought

After you have given your presentation, review what you wrote here. Which thoughts matched your experience better, the negative ones or the helpful ones? You will probably find that most of your negative thoughts were not realistic.

Visualization

Another technique you can use to improve performance is to visualize yourself giving a presentation. Visualize three different things:

- the process of giving your presentation,

- dealing with a problem during your presentation,

- completing your presentation successfully.

Exercise 9

When you have finished or almost finished preparing for your presentation, visualize yourself giving it. Follow these steps.

- Visualize standing up and walking to the front of the room. Think about the faces in the audience looking at you. Imagine starting to speak and giving your introduction.

- Visualize giving all the parts of your presentation. Imagine using your visual aids.

- Visualize the kinds of problems you could have and how you would deal with them. For example, if you are planning to show PowerPoint slides, imagine the projector not working and how you would deal with this. Imagine some members of the audience not paying attention, looking out the window, or typing on their laptops. See yourself continuing to talk calmly, even though this is happening.

- Visualize how you will feel when you complete your presentation successfully. Imagine the sense of achievement you will feel and the relief.

Doing a visualization of giving your presentation can help you build confidence. By thinking about possible problems, you will be able to deal with them better, if and when they happen. And imagining a successful outcome may help you feel more positive about the idea of giving your presentation.

Building your confidence

Glossary

pressurized
If you are in a pressurized situation or environment, you feel stressed and worried because what you have to do is difficult or you do not have much time to do it.

One of the main reasons students feel nervous is because they are worried about speaking in front of an audience. If your native language is not English, you may feel anxious about your accent, pronunciation or making mistakes.

Even if you are studying in an English-speaking country, you might not speak English very often, and certainly not in a pressurized environment. You can build up your confidence by setting yourself small speaking challenges in the weeks or days leading up to your presentation.

Exercise 10

Try the following challenges. When you complete one, put a tick next to it.

Challenge	✓
Ask somebody on the street for directions, instead of checking your phone or a map.	
Go to the library and ask for helping finding a book.	
Start a conversation about the weather with someone you have never met before.	
In a lecture or seminar, ask to borrow a pen from a student you have never spoken to before.	
Ask for a recommendation in the university canteen, cafeteria or in a restaurant.	
Make an appointment with one of your teachers to discuss something from a seminar or lecture.	
Phone or go to a bookshop and ask if they have a particular book (e.g. one from your course) and ask how much it costs.	
Make at least two contributions (expressing an opinion or asking a question) during a seminar.	
Get a haircut and have a conversation with the hairdresser.	
Call a customer services line and ask for information about a product. Ask as many questions as possible.	

When you work through this list, you can try to identify any negative thoughts you have before doing each challenge, and then see if they match your experience of doing the task.

Dealing with nerves on the day

You might feel the most nervous in the hours and minutes before your presentation. During this time, apply some of the techniques you have learned, such as replacing negative thoughts with helpful ones or visualizing giving your presentation.

However, if the nervous feelings are growing while you wait, some basic relaxation skills can be useful to help reduce the symptoms of nerves. Here are two techniques that can help you overcome your nerves, during these last moments.

Redirecting your attention

Glossary

redirect
If you redirect someone or something, you change their course or destination.

If you are feeling nervous, you may have many thoughts going around your head. You mind find it hard to control them and replace them with helpful thoughts. If this is happening, try and redirect your thoughts to something completely different.

For example, if are constantly thinking about yourself, your presentation, things you need to do, mistakes you might make and so on, redirect your thoughts to the audience. Think about what they will learn from you and how they might find the information useful.

Another common problem people have is worrying about looking nervous. When people feel nervous, they may focus on their symptoms, for example, how fast their heart is beating or how their hands are sweating or shaking. They worry that the audience will see how anxious they are and that this will create a bad impression.

However, you will almost certainly feel worse than you look. Even if the audience notices that you seem a little nervous, they cannot see how fast your heart is beating or that your hands are sweating. So focus on something away from your body. For example, watch another speaker and notice how they use their hands. It is important to direct your attention away from what is making you feel worse.

Controlled breathing

The second relaxation technique to try is controlled breathing. One of the symptoms of nervousness is fast breathing. If you lose control of your breathing, it can make you feel worse and more stressed. Try the technique in Exercise 11. Practise this technique before your presentation, so that you can do it easily on the day.

Exercise 11

Follow the instructions on controlled breathing and notice how you feel.

- First make sure your body is relaxed. Pay particular attention to your shoulders and chest.

- Close your eyes if you feel comfortable doing so. But this is not essential.

- Breathe in slowly through your nose and then out through your mouth.

- Continue breathing slowly, in through your nose and out through your mouth; count slowly from one to four in your head as you breathe in and then again, as you breathe out.

- Continue breathing like this and counting in your head. In time, you should feel your heartbeat slowing and your body relaxing.

You should be able to use this technique without other people noticing.

Remember

✓ Get everything ready in advance so you do not need to make last-minute changes while other speakers are presenting.

✓ Try to rehearse in the room where you will be presenting.

✓ Use your rehearsal to time yourself.

✓ If you are presenting in a group, in your rehearsal, focus on changeovers, visual aids and how group members behave when they are not speaking.

✓ Think about how being nervous can help you improve your performance.

✓ Replace negative thoughts with helpful ones.

✓ Use visualization and speaking challenges to build your confidence.

✓ Redirect your thoughts and control your breathing to control your nervousness on the day.

11 | Avoiding and solving problems

Aims
✓ carry out final checks
✓ resolve problems during your presentation
✓ analyse feelings after your presentation
✓ deal with questions

Aims

? Quiz
Self-evaluation

Read the statements, then circle the word which is true for you.

1	I know what final checks to do for a presentation.	agree | disagree | not sure
2	I know what to do if I have problems with the audience.	agree | disagree | not sure
3	I know some techniques to help me if I have forgotten what to say next.	agree | disagree | not sure
4	I know some language to signal to the audience that I am solving a problem.	agree | disagree | not sure
5	I can deal with questions at the end of the presentation.	agree | disagree | not sure
6	I understand how to reflect on my experiences in my presentation, so I can learn from them.	agree | disagree | not sure

If things go wrong

You have already learned about the importance of preparation and rehearsing. If you prepare your presentation thoroughly and take plenty of time to rehearse where you will give your presentation, you will probably not have any problems. Even with the best preparation, however, problems can still occur. Here are some final checks to do.

Final checks

The final checks you need to do will depend on the technology you are using for your presentation. Avoid leaving your checks until the last minute. Do them the day before, so you have time to solve any problems.

Exercise 1

Complete the advice (1–4) with the words and phrases (a–d).

a   other visual aids

b   room

c   PowerPoint presentation

d   equipment

1   Check the _____. Are there enough seats for the audience? Is the layout how you want it? Do you know where the light switches are and how to turn them on and off? Do you know how to open and close the blinds?

2   Check your _____. Have you made a final check of all the slides, looking for errors or anything you have forgotten? Do your files open on the computer you will use? Do you have a backup somewhere? (You can send yourself a backup copy as an email attachment.)

3   Check any _____. Do you have enough copies of your handouts so that every person in the audience will get one? Is there enough paper on the flipchart?

4   Check your _____. Is everything you need there? Does the computer switch on and can you log in? Can you get the computer projector working and the sound to play? Is the OHP working? Do the whiteboard or flipchart pens in the room work?

Tips ✓   Whiteboards need special pens, normally called 'dry wipe markers'. These pens do not work well on flipcharts – watercolour markers or flipchart markers are better.
✓   Check that any pens you plan to use on a whiteboard do not have the word 'permanent' written on them. This ink cannot be removed from the boards.

Problems can sometimes occur even with the best preparation. Things can happen that you cannot predict and sometimes the pressure of the situation can cause you to make mistakes. However even if you experience a problem, you can still continue and produce a very good presentation. One problem will not stop you from communicating your message.

Problems with the audience

You cannot expect to have a perfect audience. As you learned in Chapter 10, if you are presenting to the students in your seminar group, they might be talking or making last-minute changes to their own presentations. If you are presenting at a conference, people in the audience are often distracted, checking emails or walking in and out of the room.

There is very little you can do about the behaviour of the audience. Even if you are distracted, keep speaking and making eye contact with people who seem interested. Take inspiration from the people in the audience who are paying attention and do not worry about those who are not.

It is important to remember that each audience is different. You might give a presentation and find that everyone in the audience is alert, makes eye contact and seems friendly. On another occasion, you might have an audience that looks bored. Remember that the alert audience might be a confident one and the people who seem bored might just be nervous about giving their presentations after yours.

Forgetting what you want to say

In a pressurized situation, such as giving a presentation, people find that sometimes their mind 'goes blank'. This means that they completely forget what they wanted to say next. This is probably one of the most frightening problems to have – everyone in the audience is looking at you and waiting for you to speak and you simply cannot remember what to say. If this happens to you, there are several techniques you can use.

Exercise 2

Complete each piece of advice with 'Do' or 'Don't'.

1 _____ take a deep breath and try to relax. If you panic, you will find it harder to remember what you need to say.

2 _____ look at your notes. Take a few seconds to check what you have already spoken about, then decide what to move on to next.

3 _____ worry about the silence. When you start talking again, your audience will soon forget about it.

4 _____ think about the last few things you said. Sometimes, if you quickly repeat the last few key points you made (in your head or even aloud), you will remember what should come next.

5 _____ get stuck trying to think of a particular word you have forgotten. Rather, use a different word (or phrase) and continue with the presentation.

If you have rehearsed enough, you might feel on the day of your presentation that everything will be so automatic that you will not need notes. Even if you feel this confident, make sure you always have the right page of your notes visible. If your mind suddenly goes blank, you will be able to find your place again quickly.

Indicating that you have a problem

There are many small problems that can occur during a presentation. If you have a problem, it is advisable to signal that to the audience. Do Exercise 3 to learn some useful phrases for this.

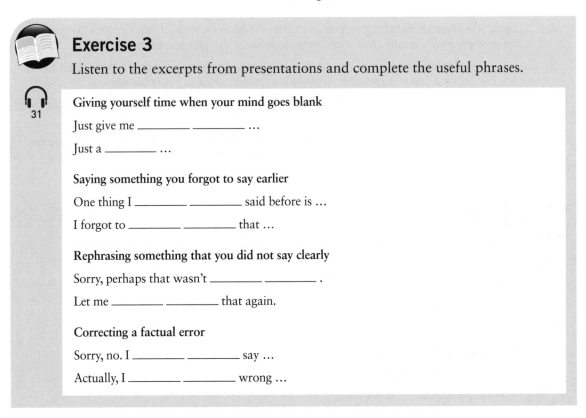

Exercise 3

Listen to the excerpts from presentations and complete the useful phrases.

31

Giving yourself time when your mind goes blank

Just give me _____ _____ …

Just a _____ …

Saying something you forgot to say earlier

One thing I _____ _____ said before is …

I forgot to _____ _____ that …

Rephrasing something that you did not say clearly

Sorry, perhaps that wasn't _____ _____ .

Let me _____ _____ that again.

Correcting a factual error

Sorry, no. I _____ _____ say …

Actually, I _____ _____ wrong …

Dealing with questions

You saw some language for asking the audience for questions in Chapter 3. Many presenters find that taking questions is one of the most enjoyable parts of giving a presentation. However, many people worry about it, normally because they are concerned about not knowing the answers to difficult questions. Look at Exercise 4 for advice about this.

Tip ✓ If you are presenting in a group, different people in the group will probably need to answer different questions, according to their area of knowledge. Choose one person in your group who will ask the audience for questions and then pass each question on to the appropriate person. This is often the person who gives the conclusion.

Exercise 4

Complete the advice with the following words.

ask	give	predict	try	worry

1 _____ which questions you might be asked. If possible, ask somebody else to watch a rehearsal of your presentation and think of possible questions.

2 _____ the audience member to repeat or explain the question again if you have not understood it. It is important to be totally clear what the person asking the question wants to know.

3 _____ yourself time to think. If you are nervous, you may immediately start talking to try to answer the question, but it is advisable to stop for a few seconds and plan your answer.

4 Do not _____ if you are not sure about the answer. It is better to say you are unsure than to give a wrong answer. However, you might like to speculate about possible answers.

5 _____ to stay calm if somebody asks a difficult question. This kind of question normally means that the person is interested in your topic and not that he or she is trying to cause you problems.

Exercise 5

Listen to the excerpts from presentations and complete the useful phrases.

32

Asking for repetition and clarification

Sorry, _____ you repeat that?

So I _____ your question is …

Giving yourself time to think

Let me _____ think about that.

Hmm, that's an _____ question.

Speculating when you do not know

It _____ be because …

I _____ it's possible that …

Managing questions in a group presentation

Juan, do you want to answer _____ one?

I think I _____ answer that one.

Feelings after your presentation

Glossary

conclude
If you conclude that something is true, you decide that it is true using the facts you know as a basis.

At the end of your presentation, you will probably have a mix of emotions. You will probably feel proud of finishing it, but also feel some relief. However, if you experienced a problem during your presentation, you might be worried or upset.

Remember that it is difficult to assess your own performance accurately. For example, if you felt very nervous, you might think that this affected your performance. However, as you know from Chapter 10, the audience does not notice most symptoms of anxiety. If you made an error and corrected yourself, you might focus on this and conclude that the presentation was a disaster. However, you should think about the whole presentation, remembering how all the parts went. Many presenters who think they gave a poor presentation often learn later from the audience that it was fine.

Give yourself a few days to reflect on your presentation, on what went well and on how you could improve in future. Use the 'Post-presentation self assessment form' on page 166 to record your thoughts. You can also ask your lecturer to give feedback on your performance. While you may officially only receive a mark or a few brief comments, you can ask for more detailed feedback.

Remember

✓ Do final checks to avoid any problems you can predict.

✓ Try not to let problems with the audience affect your performance.

✓ Learn some techniques to help you if your mind goes blank.

✓ Signal to your audience when you are dealing with a problem.

✓ Try to predict questions and do not be afraid to say you are unsure of the answer.

✓ Reflect on your final performance and how to improve in the future.

12 | Poster presentations

Quiz
Self-evaluation

Read the statements, then circle the word which is true for you.

1	I know what a poster presentation is.	agree | disagree | not sure
2	I know some advantages of poster presentations.	agree | disagree | not sure
3	I understand how to plan and choose content for a poster presentation.	agree | disagree | not sure
4	I know how to design an effective poster.	agree | disagree | not sure
5	I know what to do on the day of a poster presentation.	agree | disagree | not sure

What are poster presentations?

Glossary

field
If you say that someone fields a question, you mean that they answer it or deal with it, usually successfully.

If you are asked to give a poster presentation, your task is to produce a large poster, often summarizing and illustrating some research you have done. Normally, there is a particular day on which all students' or researchers' posters are displayed together. People who are interested can walk around, look at the different posters and ask questions about them.

Poster presentations are more common in science subjects, but are becoming more common in other disciplines, too. They are also very common at conferences. When you give a poster presentation, you normally have two tasks – first, to produce your poster and second, to stand next to it on the day, introducing it and fielding questions on it.

The advantages of poster presentations

There are many advantages to doing poster presentations. In fact, many students prefer them to normal oral presentations. Do Exercise 1 to find out about some of the advantages.

Exercise 1

Match the advantages of poster presentation, 1–4, to the explanations, a–d.

1 Poster presentations may mean more people see your work.	**a** This can be very enjoyable and is less formal than most oral presentations. You have real conversations instead of just talking and answering a few questions at the end. The information and answers you give are more specific, as you reply to the questions you are asked.
2 A poster presentation gives you the chance to talk about your work to individuals or small groups and interact more with your audience than you would in an oral presentation.	**b** After giving a poster presentation, many presenters often feel proud of the work they have produced, in contrast to oral presentations, where presenters often just feel relief that the presentation is finished.
3 Poster presentations are a good chance to get feedback on your work.	**c** As you often give a poster presentation before submitting a final written paper, feedback from a poster presentation can give you an excellent opportunity to improve your work.
4 Many presenters find giving a poster presentation a more positive experience than giving an oral presentation.	**d** If you are giving a poster presentation at a conference, more people will probably look at your poster than would see you give an oral presentation. An attractive, well-designed poster can also get the interest of people who would not normally be interested in your topic.

Choosing your content

Usually, there are two important differences between a poster presentation and the many kinds of oral presentation.

- Normally, a poster presentation is just one part of the assessment of a research project, so when you start to prepare your poster, you may already have a lot of knowledge about the topic and most of your research will already be done.

- You may not be given a specific brief for a poster presentation or a specific question to answer. You will probably just be asked to prepare a poster based on your research.

Despite these differences, many of the preparation stages for oral presentations that you learned about in Chapter 3 can be applied to poster presentations.

Exercise 2

Complete the advice about choosing content, 1–4, with the sentences, a–d.

1 _____ Make sure you know if your poster needs to contain any particular information or have a particular organization. Remember, too, that the audience is also part of this, so think about whether you will have a general or expert audience and how this could affect your choice of content.	**a** Think about which of your key ideas or findings you can present visually, instead of with text.
2 _____ If you are working on a larger research project, you might be able to make a list of a number of different areas you could make into a poster.	**b** Think about all the different messages you could communicate in your poster.
3 _____ Try to think of a single message you want to share with your audience, and choose only the related ideas that you feel you must include to communicate it successfully. Give priority to conclusions and recommendations and avoid too much detail on methods and results.	**c** Analyse your brief.
4 _____ You should try to present as much information as you can with images, tables, graphs and so on, and use as little text as possible.	**d** Choose one message you want to communicate and decide on the key ideas you need to include.

The importance of visual content

It is important to understand that poster presentations should be mainly *visual*. You learned that when you give an oral presentation, the visual aids should only support the message that you are communicating when you speak. A poster presentation is very different. Your poster should communicate your message for you and you only need to speak, when introducing it and fielding questions.

Students often make the mistake of including too much content, particularly too much text. A poster presentation is not a document, like an essay or an article. Explain as much as possible with your visuals (graphs, maps, illustrations or photographs) instead of with your text and only include details specifically needed to communicate your message. Be very selective about the content you include. You will normally be present to field questions, when you can explain things in more detail if necessary.

Tip ✓ Leave some blank space on your poster instead of filling every part. Blank space can make a poster easier to read and more attractive.

Exercise 3

Choose 'Do' or 'Don't' to complete the advice on the content of poster presentations.

1 *Do / Don't* use images as much as possible to communicate your message.

2 *Do / Don't* use a lot of dense text.

3 *Do / Don't* give lots of detail on methods and results.

4 *Do / Don't* focus on conclusions and recommendations.

5 *Do / Don't* try to focus on one main message.

6 *Do / Don't* make the message of your poster clear.

Tip

Tip ✓ Choose a title that gives a clear message. For example, instead of 'The effect of educational programmes on fitness in high school children', choose 'Educational programmes improve fitness in high school children'.

Creating your poster

You should spend a lot more time on producing your poster presentation than on your visual aids for an oral presentation. Your poster *is* your presentation, so it is worth giving yourself a lot of time to make it as effective and attractive as possible. Take care to follow all the instructions you have been given for your presentation.

Basic design

Glossary

landscape
Landscape is the way of printing a document in which the top and bottom of the page are longer than the sides.

portrait
Portrait is the way of printing a document in which the sides of the page are longer than the top and bottom.

First find out about the basic rules for your poster. Make sure you know:

- how much space you will have for it and if the poster must be a specific size,

- what basic information you need to include and where it should appear,

- if you should organize the poster in a particular way, such as using standard headings.

If you are giving a poster presentation for your course, there may be a standard PowerPoint template that you should use to create your poster. This may include information such as the university logo and your course title.

Tips ✓ A typical organization for a scientific poster presentation is: title, summary, introduction, theory and methodology, results, conclusion and further work. Find out if you should do yours differently, however.

✓ Remember that you need to use citations and include a reference, just as you do for any written assignment. See appendix 3 – Citations and references on page 162 for advice on citation, but remember you should follow the guidelines at your university.

Tips

Before you start creating your poster, you need to choose one of two basic methods: creating a poster on one large piece of paper or using a combination of several smaller sheets of paper. Sometimes you will be asked to produce a poster on a single sheet of paper, but often the choice is yours. Each method has advantages and disadvantages.

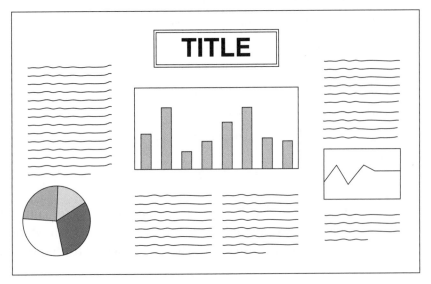

A poster on a single, large sheet of paper

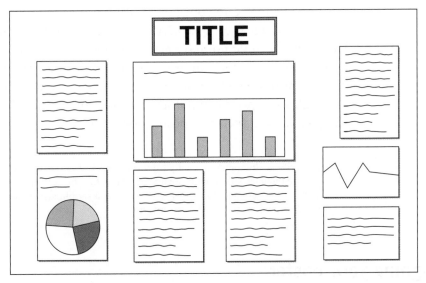

A poster on a several smaller sheets of paper

Exercise 4

Read the list of advantages and disadvantages and decide whether each refers to a) a single large poster or b) a poster made of several smaller sheets of paper.

1 It is easier to put up, take down, store and transport. _____
2 It can look untidy, especially if reused several times. _____
3 It is cheaper and easier to print, as you can use any printer. _____
4 It is easier to change the organization and order. _____
5 It is expensive to print and can only be produced with a professional printer. _____
6 It looks more professional and attractive. _____
7 Its organization cannot be changed once printed. _____
8 It takes more time to put up. _____

You need to decide whether to make your poster landscape or portrait. Sometimes you will have no choice. So find out how much space you will have for your poster and whether a specific format is required.

Software

It is possible to create your poster using professional design software, such as InDesign® or QuarkXPress to design and lay out your poster. However, if you do not have access to these programs or do not know how to use them, you can use PowerPoint or other presentation software. You can also use a word-processing programme, like Microsoft Word, although some people find it less suitable for creating documents with a complex layout, such as a poster presentation.

Tip ✓ PowerPoint slides automatically print out on A4 or letter-sized paper. Make sure you change the page size of your document so it is the correct size for a large poster. A0 is 118.9 × 84.1 cm and A1 is 84.1 × 59.4 cm. You should also choose whether you want the document to be landscape or portrait.

Designing your poster

Your poster needs to be attractive for people to want to stop and read it. At the same time, it needs to be informative and easy to follow. In the following sections, you will look at how to combine these two features.

The reading path and your basic poster organization

The 'reading path' is the direction your eyes follow when you read. Normally, with a document that is mostly text, this is simple. In English, we start at the top and then read from left to right, line by line, until we get to the bottom. With a poster, however, the reading path is more complex.

The reading path you choose must be logical and obvious to the person viewing your poster. You need to help your audience understand how to read your poster. The standard reading path for landscape and portrait posters is shown by the arrows below:

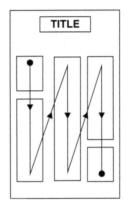

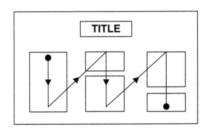

Reading path in a landscape poster   Reading path in a portrait poster

There are many other variations of reading paths you can use. Remember, however, that the simpler the reading path, the better for your audience. In particular, note that it is often difficult to read long, wide lines of text. Make sure that you use columns of text, instead of lines of text that run across the whole page.

Tip ✓ To make the reading path clear on your poster, you can add arrows between sections or give each section a number. This will help people know where to read next.

Font size and type

In Chapter 9, you learned about the importance of using a suitable font size and type for a PowerPoint presentation. The same is true for a poster. All the sections of your poster should be readable from two steps back. For this reason, do not use a font of less than 24 point size for the sections with text. If your text cannot fit at 24 point, you probably have too much. To make your text shorter, you could present some of it in bullet points, with just the key words. Review what you learned in Chapter 4 about choosing key words.

Titles and headings

Titles and headings should be much larger than your text. Your main title should be readable from more than five steps away, so it can be easily read from a distance. Section headings should be smaller than your title, but bigger than any text sections. Be consistent with the size of your headings.

Much of the other advice you read about in Chapter 9 is important for poster design. Do Exercise 5 to review what you have learned.

Exercise 5

Complete the summary of things to remember when designing your poster with the following words and phrases.

difficult	sans serif	serif	two	two or three	appropriate

Firstly, choose a font that is **1**_____ to an academic context. Avoid using Comic sans serif or any fonts that do not look serious or are **2**_____ to read. Do not use more than **3**_____ font types – choose one font and use it for all your headings, and choose another font and use it for all other text.

For long sections of text, **4**_____ fonts like Times New Roman are easier to read. However, if you just use key words, **5**_____ fonts like Arial are generally better. Be careful with your choice of colour. Limit yourself to **6**_____ different colours and choose either shades of a single colour, or complementary colours, like red with green, or blue with orange.

Tips

Tips ✓ Remember what you learned about using photographs and clip art. Use only images that are appropriate for an academic presentation.

✓ Choose high-quality images that will not be distorted when printed or displayed large. Images should be at least 200 dpi and you should not enlarge them. You can normally find out the dpi by right-clicking on an image, choosing 'Properties' then 'Details'.

Final checks

Glossary

readability
The readability of a document is how clear and easy it is to read.

anonymous
If you remain anonymous when you do something, you do not let people know that you were the person who did it.

If you are creating a poster on a single piece of paper, you can check the readability by printing a small version on a letter-size piece of paper and putting it on a wall. Take one step back and see if you can read it – if you cannot, you need to make some changes.

Ask for feedback from friends, fellow students or colleagues. If possible, print out a full-sized copy of the poster and ask people to come and comment on it, by writing directly on the poster or making notes. It is best if you leave the room when they do this, so their feedback can be anonymous.

On the day of the presentation

On the day of the poster presentation, you normally need to stand next to your presentation so you can introduce it and answer questions. At a conference, you will not be present all the time. However, if you have produced a poster for your course, you may need to stand next to the poster for the whole session.

Find out in advance how you will put up your poster. In some situations, you will be expected to bring your own pins to put it up and in others, you will need to use Velcro. Make sure you arrive early so you have time to resolve any difficulties.

Tip

Tip ✓ If you made your poster from separate sheets of paper, make sure that you align the different sheets correctly. Step away from your poster and check from a distance if they are straight. It can be difficult to check alignment if you are very close.

Introducing your poster

It is really important to spend some time preparing how you will introduce your presentation. When introducing a poster, you should not read from notes, as your introduction should be very short. Think about how you can introduce the main ideas in an interesting way, in less than a minute.

Just like when you give an oral presentation, make sure you face your audience and not your poster when you are talking and answering questions. Your body should always be turned towards the people you are speaking to. Move your gaze between them and your poster. Look again at what you learned about body language in Chapter 6 for help with this.

Exercise 6

Listen to someone introducing a poster. Complete their introduction with the following useful phrases (a–e).

33

introducing your poster

a   The idea is that …

b   My poster shows …

c   The results we found from this were …

d   This has implications for …

e   We looked at …

1 _____ how educational programmes can have a positive effect on the fitness of high school children. 2 _____ that by providing education on the importance of fitness and giving advice on exercise, you can encourage high school children to improve fitness on their own. 3 _____ one school here in the local area and found out about the exercise habits of children before and after the programme.

4 _____ that children exercised more after attending the programme, as you can see here. 5 _____ educational policy-makers and could be important for the fight against the increasing amount of obesity in the country.

Getting the most from the experience

Giving a poster presentation can be an excellent way to make contacts and network. Try to be proactive – when somebody comes to see your poster, ask them their name and what they do. You can often meet people during a poster presentation that can help you with your studies or work. You might meet professionals that you can collaborate with in the future. You can also leave a visitors book at your poster, where people can write their contact details.

It is advisable to prepare something to give to people who come to see your poster. If you have already written an abstract, keep copies of that. You might make a handout, summarizing the key parts of your presentation. If you made your poster on a single sheet of paper, you can print out smaller copies to give to people. Make sure that anything you give out is easy to read. Some presenters also prepare business cards with their contact details to give out.

Remember

✓ Try to communicate a single message and choose your content carefully.

✓ Make sure your poster communicates your message as visually as possible.

✓ Make your poster effective and attractive by choosing layout, fonts and colours carefully.

✓ Prepare a short, spoken introduction to give to people who are interested in your poster.

✓ Find out about the people viewing your poster as they may be useful contacts.

✓ Prepare a handout to give to people who view your poster.

Appendix 1 – Useful phrases

Useful phrases that you have been introduced to throughout the book are reproduced here in Appendix 1 for easy reference.

Expressing ideas

- I think (it's sort of old fashioned to think of the internet like that).
- I would say that (there are a lot of reasons why the cold war ended).
- In my view, (we need to think about parenting in a different context).
- In my opinion, (the policy might work better in the developed world).
- It seems to me that (most governments in the world aren't interested in stopping climate change).

Hedging

- It seems (that most governments in the world aren't interested in stopping climate change).
- Perhaps (we need to think about parenting in a different context).
- (The policy) might (work better in the developed world).
- I'd say (there are a lot of reasons why the cold war ended).
- In a sense, (both writers are making the same point about modernism).
- Maybe (stable prices are impossible in the economy at the moment).
- (I think,) in a way, (that looking at human rights as universal isn't always right).
- (I think it's) sort of (old-fashioned to think of the internet like that).

Explaining reasons

- One reason for (that) is (people don't have confidence in the product).
- (This reaction) happens because (the two liquids react to each other).
- That's (the reason) why (the political problems began).
- That's because (not enough research has been done yet).
- One explanation (of his popularity) is (the power of the media).

Finishing what you were saying

- Just to finish what I was saying before, (I think the writer makes an interesting point about food distribution).
- That's true, but what I wanted to say was (you've got to consider what else was happening at the time to really understand why the war started).
- Can I just finish what I was saying before?

Justifying a request

- I was wondering, (how this kind of thing affects a country's exports)?
- I'm just curious if (the temples also had an economic function).
- Just out of interest, (how much was Verdi influenced by Meyerbeer)?

Linking to an earlier contribution

- Earlier you said (we need to think about two things).
- You mentioned before that (the article isn't the most up to date).
- Just thinking about your previous point, (is it right to think that Hobbes and Locke completely disagree about human nature)?

Asking for more information about what you have understood

- Could you expand on what you mean when you say (the article contradicts itself)?
- Can you just explain why (he said that)?
- You say that (Smith felt that people are self interested). How does this (relate to the idea of people being sympathetic)?
- When you say ('most of the time'), what exactly do you mean?
- Could you just repeat the point about (the strikes in the 1970s)?

Paraphrasing

- So do you mean that (the results are totally conclusive)?
- So does the writer mean that (the profits were hidden)?
- So you're saying that (there were other reasons, too)?
- So what the writer is saying is that (the separation of state and religion was inevitable)?
- So in other words, (the policy failed).
- So the point is that (you can't really prove there's a relationship between the two things).

Agreeing and adding your thoughts

- I agree with that because (it matches my experience).
- I think that's true for another reason – (something we talked about in the last seminar).
- Yeah, and also because (the state had more control in those days).

Disagreeing indirectly

- (Not all of the Millennium Development Goals are easy to achieve,) though.
- That's true, but (I also think the other treatment options are important).
- Don't you think (that governments should invest more during periods like this)?
- (Companies like this don't have much chance of success,) do they?

Introducing the topic

- The topic I want to talk about today is (problems countries in the developing world have with exporting goods).
- This morning I'm going to focus on (problems countries in the developing world have with exporting goods).
- Today I'm going to outline and discuss (problems countries in the developing world have with exporting goods).

Getting the audience interested

- One thing you might not know about (exports from the developing world) is (that developing countries obtain 32 times as much revenue from exports as they do from aid).
- Did you know that (developing countries obtain 32 times as much revenue from exports as they do from aid)?
- Have you ever thought about why (countries in the developing world are unable to export easily to the US and the EU)?

Giving the structure of your presentation

- I'm first going to (talk about the kind of goods exported). / Then I'm going to (look at the restrictions they face). / Finally, I'm going to (look at the positive effects that a small increase on exports could have).
- I'm going to start by looking at (the kinds of goods exported by developing countries). / Then I'll move on to (restrictions they face from the US and the EU). / To finish, I'll talk to you about (the positive effects that a small increase on exports could have).
- My presentation is divided into three parts. First, (I'm going to talk about the kinds of goods exported by developing countries). / Second, (I'm going to look at restrictions they face from the US and the EU). / Third, (I'm going to talk about the positive effects that a small increase in exports could have).

Referring to sources

- According to (Massarelli, there were three main reasons).
- (Karlson) says that (all these things are untestable).
- (Shorey) argues that (previous studies got it wrong).
- (Dewaele)'s theory is that (the policies worked).
- Here you can see Durkheim's definition of (the 'social facts').

Repeating the main points

- In conclusion, we looked at (the kinds of goods exported, the restrictions they face and the positive effects of a small increase on exports).
- I'd like to conclude by reviewing (the main points of the presentation).

Saying what the main argument or conclusion was

- And I argued that (developing countries are really being held back by trade restrictions).
- I hoped to show that (we can't expect improvements unless the policy is changed).

Thanking the audience

- Thank you for listening.
- Thanks for your attention.

Leaving the audience with an interesting thought or idea

- The important thing for us to think about now is (how we can improve the situation).
- So, what would you do if (you were a policy-maker in the EU)?
- I'd like to finish by (reading you a quotation from Keynes).

Asking for questions

- Are there any questions?
- Does anybody have a question?

Moving from part to part in a group

- Now Sara is going to talk about (the results of the survey).
- Next, Mehmet will move on to (possible solutions).
- Xu Li is now going to look at (the most important implications).

Referring to visual aids

- As you can see in this table, (there are four key periods).
- This graph shows (the results of the test).
- If you look at this slide, what you can see is (an increase in the number of bankruptcies in the period).
- Have a look at this graph.
- If we move on to the next slide (we can see why this happens).
- I'd like you to look at this table, which shows (all the different figures from the two countries).

Talking about visual aids you have shown or will show

- We'll come to that in the next table.
- We'll see some graphs about that later.
- I'll explain why in the next few graphs.
- I'm going to show you some slides about (the development of the residential area).
- Remember that quote right at the beginning (about possible causes).
- We'll come back to this table later in the presentation.

Focusing on a visual aid

- If you just look at (the left part of the chart, you can see that the number of young people staying on beyond 16 has increased in that ten-year period).
- But take a closer look at (the centre part).
- Now focus on (the part on the right).

Explaining the message in a visual aid

- What this shows us is (that while there are fewer people leaving school at 16, there are also fewer people staying in education at 18).
- The message here is that (in Europe the brand is much less popular than it used to be).
- Looking at this, we can say that (the policy didn't really work).
- This is important, because (it was only after this meeting that things really started to happen).
- What this highlights is that (not all verbs behave in the same way).

Presenting

Giving yourself time when your mind goes blank

- Just give me a second (to think about that).
- Just a moment, where was I?

Saying something you forgot to say earlier

- One thing I should have said before is (that some of the respondents didn't answer all the questions).
- I forgot to say earlier that (when we looked at the two together, there seemed to be a relationship).

Rephrasing something that you did not say clearly

- Sorry, perhaps that wasn't very clear. The important thing is (that the results showed that the advertising was a success).
- Let me just explain that again. What you can see here is (the situation before and after the treatment).

Correcting a factual error

- Sorry, no. I meant to say (that not all of the products were ready at that point).
- Actually, I got that wrong. It's (the first number, not the second number that you need to remember).

Asking for repetition and clarification

- Sorry, could you repeat that?
- So I think your question is (about whether or not this could be applied to other contexts).

Giving yourself time to think

- Let me just think about that.
- Hmm, that's an interesting question.

Speculating when you do not know

- It might be because (there were more than three different nationality groups tested).
- I suppose it's possible that (they didn't know what would happen in a situation like that).

Managing questions in a group presentation

- Juan, do you want to answer that one?
- I think I can answer that one.

Introducing your poster

- The idea is that (by providing education on the importance of fitness, you can encourage children to improve fitness on their own).
- My poster shows (how educational programmes can have a positive effect on the fitness of children).
- The results we found from this were (that children exercised more after attending the programme).
- This has implications for (educational policy makers).
- We looked at (one school here in the local area).

Appendix 2 – Talking about numbers and figures

This appendix contains useful phrases you can use to talk about numbers and figures during your presentation. It also gives an overview of some different ways of presenting numbers and figures visually.

Comparing figures

Similarity:
- The figures for group A and group B were **exactly the same**.
- There were **as many** positive responses **as** negative responses.
- There was **no difference between** the figures in the two periods.
- The number of 'yes' votes **was similar** in both years.

Difference:
- There were **more** occurrences in 2011 **than** in 2012.
- There was **less** interest **than** in previous years.
- **Fewer** accidents occurred in Europe **than** in the USA.
- There were **double / three times / four times** the number of 'yes' responses **as** 'no' responses.

Talking about change

Increases:
- There was a **rise in** prices.
- Prices **rose by** 20 per cent.

Decreases:
- There was **a fall in** prices.
- Prices **fell by** 20 per cent.
- There was a drop in levels of satisfaction.
- Levels of satisfaction dropped.

Maximums and minimums:
- The pass rate **reached a high** in the following decade.
- Prices **peaked** in 2010.
- Prices **hit rock bottom** in 2011.
- Sales **bottomed out** after the crisis hit.

Making changes stronger:
- There was a **dramatic** drop in prices here.
- The values dropped **dramatically** later in the year.
- Look at the **massive** increase in this year.
- The number of people in higher education increased **massively** during the 1960s.

Presenting

Making changes weaker:

- There were some **gradual** improvements in performances as a result.
- The number of cars dropped **gradually** during the period.
- We can see a **slight** increase here.
- The values changed **slightly**, but it doesn't seem significant.

Changing:

- The birth rate **fluctuated** between 1980 and 1985.
- Inflation **went up and down** during the period.
- House prices **were unsteady** over the five-year period.
- Market values **showed a lot of variation** throughout the day.

No change:

- Employment **remained stable** in the 1950s.
- Crime **levelled off** after those earlier increases.
- There were **no changes** in this part.
- The value here **stays level** despite changes elsewhere.

Speaking approximately:

- There were **just over** 200 responses.
- We interviewed **just under** 150 people.
- The study took place over **more or less** three months.
- The final figure was **about** 250,000.

In presentations, speakers normally approximate figures when speaking, for example saying 'about eight' instead of '7.94'. However, key figures in the presentation – especially if it is new information that has been discovered from research – are normally spoken precisely.

Charts, graphs and tables

Presenting numbers

There are many different ways to present numbers in a visual aid. The type you choose will depend on what you are trying to show. Here are four of the most common types.

Pie chart

A pie chart shows percentages of a total amount. For example, you could use a pie chart to show the percentage of people that answered 'yes', 'no' and 'not sure' to a question. Pie charts are generally attractive and give a quick and clear visual representation of numbers. They are not the best choice when you have many different categories, or categories with very small percentages (as these may not be easy to see in the chart). Pie charts also do not give exact numerical data and it is can be difficult to compare two pie charts.

Bar graph

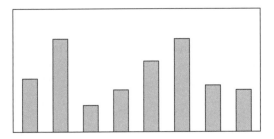

A bar graph shows data in separate columns. For example, you could use a bar chart to show the percentage of people in a country that owned a car in different time periods. Bar graphs are a good way of comparing different sets of figures and are visually attractive and clear.

Line graph

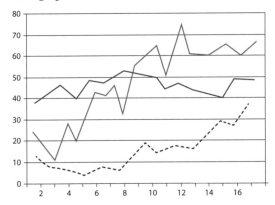

A line graph shows data using a single line. For example, you could use a line graph to show the unemployment rate in a country over a period of time. Line graphs are best for showing continuous data, for example changes over time. Since a line graph can show more than one line, they are useful for comparing two different sets of data.

Table

UN Member States	
Member	**Date joined**
Bangladesh	1974
Bhutan	1971
India	1945
Myanmar	1948
Nepal	1955
Pakistan	1947
Sri Lanka	1955

A table is used to show numbers and other text in rows and columns. Tables are good for showing a number of different figures together, and they display the exact data. The disadvantages are that they do not display information visually, so in a presentation the presenter and/or audience may have to make their own analysis. They are not always very visually attractive, especially if they are very large.

Appendix 3 – Citations and references

This is a basic guide to the American Psychological Association (APA) citation style. Check with your university which citation style you should use, as it may be different.

Citations in text

Single author:

Give the author surname and year of publication.

- According to Jones (2010), ...
- One study found this not to be true (Jones 2010).

Two authors:

Give both author surnames and year. If the surnames are part of your sentence in the text, link the names with 'and'. If they are in brackets, use '&'.

- According to Jones and Thompson (2010), ...
- One study found this not to be true (Jones & Thompson 2010).

More than two authors:

Give all author surnames and year the first time. If the surnames are part of your sentence in the text, link the names with 'and'. If they are in brackets, use '&'.

- According to Jones, Thompson and Marks (2010), ...
- One study found this not to be true (Jones, Thompson & Marks 2010).

If you use the same reference later, just use the first surname followed by 'et al', and then the year.

- Jones et al (2010) also found that ...
- Later studies confirmed the result (Jones et al 2010).

If the author is an organization or an institute, use its name.

- According to the Institute of Psychiatry (2008), ...

If there is no author name, use the first two or three words of the title.

Reference list

A reference list should be organized in alphabetical order, by the surname of the title. Do not number the list or use bullet points.

For books, use the following order of information:

author surname(s), initial (year). *Title*. Place of publication: Publisher

- Dorst, K. (2006). *Understanding Design*. Amsterdam: BIS Publishers

For a chapter in an edited book with many authors, use the following order of information:

chapter author surname(s), initial. (year). Title of chapter. In editor initial(s), surname(s) (Ed.). *Title*. Place of publication: Publisher

- Gopnik, M. (1992) When language is a problem. In R. Campbell (Ed.), *Mental Lives*. Oxford: Blackwell

For a journal article, use the following order of information:

author surname(s), initial (year). Title of article. *Name of journal*, volume (issue number). page numbers

- De Bot, K. 2004. The multilingual lexicon: modelling selection and control. *International Journal of Multilingualism*, 1(1). 17–32.

Plagiarism

Plagiarism is academic cheating. It means using somebody else's words or work without saying you have done so. Many students plagiarize unintentionally because they do not know what plagiarism is.

Some examples of plagiarism in the context of an academic presentation are:

- using a definition found on the internet, for example on a site like Wikipedia, without saying where the definition comes from,
- scanning a graph or chart from a book and using it in a visual aid, without saying where it comes from,
- using your own words to talk about something you have read, without saying where you read it.

At English-medium universities, plagiarism is generally considered extremely serious. Punishments can often include failing a course or module, or even expulsion from the university.

To avoid plagiarism, remember these key points:

- If you use the exact words from another source, e.g. a book or website, use quotation marks and include a citation to show where the words come from. Citations should also be included in visual aids.
- If you use an illustration, chart, table, etc. from another source, include a citation to show where the words come from. Again, this includes any visual aids you use.
- If you mention ideas, theories, results, etc. from another source, include a citation to show where they come from. Even if you use your own words, you still need to do this.

Appendix 4 – Presentation outline (completed)

This shows a completed outline template used to plan a presentation on high-speed rail. You can use the blank template on the next page to help plan the ideas for your presentation. There are four sections but if your presentation is divided up into more sections you can make more photocopies.

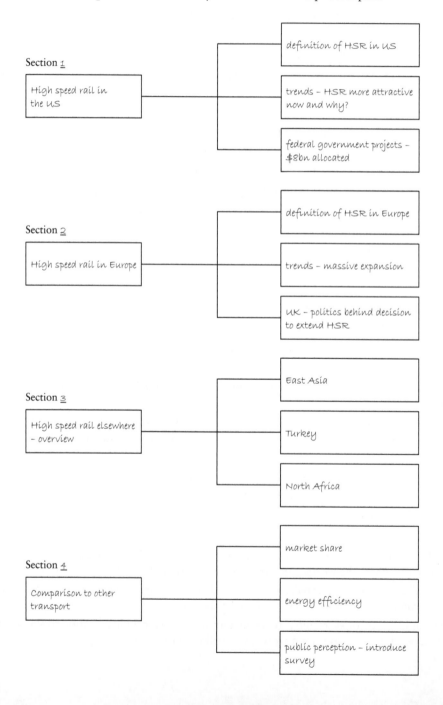

Section 1

High speed rail in the US

- definition of HSR in US
- trends – HSR more attractive now and why?
- federal government projects – $8bn allocated

Section 2

High speed rail in Europe

- definition of HSR in Europe
- trends – massive expansion
- UK – politics behind decision to extend HSR

Section 3

High speed rail elsewhere – overview

- East Asia
- Turkey
- North Africa

Section 4

Comparison to other transport

- market share
- energy efficiency
- public perception – introduce survey

Presentation outline template

Title of presentation _____

Section ___

Section ___

Section ___

Section ___

Appendix 5 – Post-presentation self assessment form

What went well:

What didn't go well:

How I could improve this next time:

Glossary of grammatical terms

adjective
An adjective is a word such as 'big', 'dead', or 'financial' that describes a person or thing, or gives extra information about them. Adjectives usually come before nouns or after link verbs.

adverb
An adverb is a word such as 'slowly', 'now', 'very', 'politically', or 'fortunately' which adds information about the action, event, or situation mentioned in a clause.

article
In grammar, an article is a kind of determiner. In English, 'a' and 'an' are called the indefinite article, and 'the' is called the definite article.

clause
In grammar, a clause is a group of words containing a verb. Sentences contain one or more clauses.

noun
A noun is a word such as 'car', 'love', or 'Anne' which is used to refer to a person or thing.

object
In grammar, the object of a verb or a preposition is the word or phrase which completes the structure begun by the verb or preposition.

preposition
A preposition is a word such as 'by', 'for', 'into', or 'with' which usually has a noun group as its object.

question tag
In grammar, a question tag is a very short clause at the end of a statement which changes the statement into a question. For example, in 'She said half price, didn't she?', the words 'didn't she' are a question tag.

subject
In grammar, the subject of a clause is the noun group that refers to the person or thing that is doing the action expressed by the verb. For example, in 'My cat keeps catching birds', 'my cat' is the subject.

that clause
In grammar, a *that* clause is a clause beginning with the word 'that'. For example, in 'I knew that was the problem', 'that was the problem' is a *that* clause.

verb
A verb is a word such as 'sing', 'feel', or 'die' which is used with a subject to say what someone or something does or what happens to them, or to give information about them.

wh- clause
In grammar, a *wh-* clause is a clause beginning with a *wh-* word, such as 'where', 'who' and 'which'. For example, in 'They are deciding where to go', 'where to go' is a *wh-* clause.

Glossary

Some of the more difficult words from the chapters are defined here in this Glossary. The definitions focus on the meanings of the words in the context in which they appear in the text. Definitions are from *COBUILD Advanced Dictionary*.

Key

ADJ	adjective	N-UNCOUNT	uncount noun
ADV	adverb	N-VAR	variable noun
AUX	auxiliary verb	NEG	negative
COLOUR	colour word	NUM	number
COMB	combining form	ORD	ordinal
CONJ	conjunction	PASSIVE	see V-PASSIVE
CONVENTION	convention	PHRASAL VERB	phrasal verb
DET	determiner	PHRASE	phrase
EXCLAM	exclamation	PREDET	predeterminer
FRACTION	fraction	PREFIX	prefix
LINK	see V-LINK	PREP	preposition
MODAL	modal verb	PRON	pronoun
N-COUNT	count noun	QUANT	quantifier
N-PLURAL	plural noun	QUEST	question word
N-PROPER	proper noun	SUFFIX	suffix
N-PROPER-PLURAL	plural proper noun	VERB	verb
N-SING	singular noun	V-LINK	link verb
N-TITLE	title noun	V-PASSIVE	passive verb

a

abstract (abstracts) N-COUNT
An abstract of an article, document, or speech is a short piece of writing, that gives the main points of it.

achievement (achievements) N-COUNT
An achievement is something which someone has succeeded in doing, especially after a lot of effort.

alert ADJ
If you are alert, you are paying full attention to things around you and are able to deal with anything that might happen

aloud ADV [ADV after v]
When you say something, read, or laugh aloud, you speak or laugh so that other people can hear you.

anonymous ADJ
If you remain anonymous when you do something, you do not let people know that you were the person who did it.

anticipation N-UNCOUNT
Anticipation is a feeling of excitement about something pleasant or exciting that you know is going to happen

assess (assesses, assessing, assessed) VERB
When you assess a person, thing, or situation, you consider them in order to make a judgment about them.

assignment (assignments) N-COUNT
An assignment is a task or piece of work that you are given to do, especially as part of your job or studies.

automatic ADJ

An automatic machine or device is one which has controls that enable it to perform a task without needing it to be constantly operated by a person.

b

blind (blinds) N-COUNT

A blind is a covering made of cloth, paper, plastic, or metal which you can pull down over a window.

brief (briefs) N-COUNT

If someone gives you a brief, they give you detailed instructions on how to complete a task.

bullet point (bullet points) N-COUNT

A bullet point is one of a series of important items for discussion or action in a document, usually marked by a square or round symbol.

bump into PHRASAL VERB [INFORMAL]

If you bump into something or someone, you accidentally hit them while you are moving.

by heart PHRASE

If you know something such as a poem by heart, you have learned it so well that you can remember it without having to read it.

c

casual ADJ

If you are casual, you are, or you pretend to be, relaxed and not very concerned about what is happening or what you are doing.

change of turn (changes of turn) N-VAR

A change of turn happens when one person stops talking and another begins.

cite (cites, citing, cited) VERB

If you cite something, you quote it, or mention it, especially as an example or proof of what you are saying.

clash (clashes, clashing, clashed) VERB

If one colour or style clashes with another, the colours or styles look ugly together. You can also say that two colours or styles clash.

cognitive psychologist (cognitive psychologists) N-COUNT

A cognitive psychologist studies how people think, remember, speak, and perceive.

commonplace ADJ

If something is commonplace, it happens often or is often found, and is therefore not surprising.

conclude (concludes, concluding, concluded) VERB

If you conclude that something is true, you decide that it is true using the facts you know as a basis.

consequences (consequence) N-COUNT

The consequences of something are the results or the effects of it.

consistent ADJ

If a book or document is consistent, it has a similar style or appearance throughout.

content (contents) N-PLURAL

If you refer to the content or contents of something such as a book, speech, or television programme, you are referring to the subject that it deals with, or the ideas that it expresses.

contract (contracts, contracting, contracted) VERB

When something contracts or when something contracts it, it becomes smaller or shorter.

convenience N-UNCOUNT

If something is done for your convenience, it is done in a way that is useful or suitable for you.

convention (conventions) N-VAR

A convention is a way of behaving that is corrected to be correct or polite by most people in a society.

corridor (corridors) N-COUNT

A transport corridor is a long narrow area of land that follows the course of a road, railway, river, or canal.]

course requirements N-PLURAL

The requirements of a course are the things that a student needs to do and the subjects and classes that they must take when studying a particular course.

criteria N-COUNT

Plural for criterion

A criterion is a factor on which you judge or decide something.

crop (crops, cropping, cropped) VERB

If you crop a photograph or image, you cut off part of it.

Presenting

d

dedicate (dedicates, dedicating, dedicated) VERB
If you dedicate time to something, you spend time doing it.

delay (delays) N-COUNT
If there is a delay, something does not happen until later than planned or expected.

diligent ADJ
Someone who is diligent works hard in a careful and thorough way.

disadvantage (disadvantages) N-COUNT
A disadvantage is a factor which makes someone or something less useful, acceptable, or successful than other people or things.

distinction (distinctions) N-COUNT
A distinction between similar things is a difference.

distinguish (distinguishes, distinguishing, distinguished) VERB
If you can distinguish one thing from another or distinguish between two things, you can see or understand how they are different.

distract (distracts, distracting, distracted) VERB
If something distracts you or your attention from something, it takes your attention away from it.

dizzy (dizzier, dizziest) ADJ
If you feel dizzy, you feel that you are losing your balance and are about to fall.

drag
To drag a computer image means to use the mouse to move the position of the image on the screen, or to change its size or shape.

durable ADJ
Something that is durable is strong and lasts a long time without breaking or becoming weaker.

e

effective ADJ
Something that is effective works well and produces the results that were intended.

emphasize (emphasizes, emphasizing, emphasized) [in BRIT, also use emphasise] VERB
To emphasize something means to indicate that it is particularly important or true, or to draw special attention to it.

emphatic ADJ
An emphatic response or statement is one made in a forceful way, because the speaker feels very strongly about what they are saying.

engage (engages, engaging, engaged) VERB
If something or someone engages you or your attention or interest, they keep you interested in them and thinking about them.

English-medium ADJ
If a school or university is English-medium, then English is the language used for teaching there.

enlarge (enlarges, enlarging, enlarged) VERB
When you enlarge something or when it enlarges, it becomes bigger.

equivalent ADJ
If one amount or value is the equivalent of another, they are the same.

explicitly ADV [ADV with v. ADV adj]
If you do something explicitly, you express or show it clearly and openly, without any attempt to hide anything.

f

factual ADJ
Something that is factual is concerned with facts or contains facts, rather than giving theories or personal interpretations.

field (fields, fielding, fielded) VERB
If you say that something fields a question, you mean that they answer it or deal with it, usually successfully.

final assessment N-VAR
Your final assessment is the final mark or grade you get from your lecturer, after you have completed all the parts of a course.

font (fonts) N-COUNT
In printing and graphics, a font is a set of characters with the same style and appearance in all its letters of the alphabet and numbers, e.g. Times New Roman.

g

gaze N-COUNT
Your gaze is the direction in which you look with your eyes.

Glossary

gesture (gestures) N-COUNT
A gesture is a movement that you make with a part of your body, especially your hands, to express emotion or information.

glance (glances, glancing, glanced) VERB
If you glance at something or someone, you look at them very quickly and then look away again immediately.

h

hand in PHRASAL VERB
If you hand in something such as homework or something that you have found, you give it to a teacher, a police officer, or other person in authority.

handbook (handbooks) N-COUNT
A handbook is a book that gives you advice and instructions about a particular subject.

highlight (highlights) VERB
highlight (highlights, highlighting, highlighted) VERB
If someone or something highlights a point or problem, they emphasize it or make you think about it.

hypothesis (hypotheses) N-VAR
A hypothesis is an idea which is suggested as a possible explanation for a particular situation or condition, but which has not yet been proved to be correct.

i

in advance PHRASE
If you do something in advance, you do it before a particular date or event.

inspiration (inspirations) N-UNCOUNT
Inspiration is a feeling of enthusiasm you get from someone or something, which gives you new and creative ideas.

interact (interacts, interacting, interacted) VERB
When people interact with each other or interact, they communicate as they work or spend time together.

intonation (intonations) N-VAR
Your intonation is the way that your voice rises and falls as you speak.

k

knowledgeable ADJ
Someone who is knowledgeable has or shows a clear understanding of many different facts about the world or about a particular subject.

l

landscape N-UNCOUNT
Landscape is the way of printing a document in which the top and bottom of the page are longer than the sides

layout N-COUNT
The layout of a garden, building, or piece of writing is the way in which the parts of it are arranged.

literature review (literature reviews) N-COUNT
If you do a literature review, you read relevant literature such as books and journal articles so that you have a good, basic knowledge of a topic.

m

metaphorical ADJ
You use the word metaphorical to indicate that you are not using words, images, or actions with their ordinary meaning, but are describing something by means of an image or symbol.

method (methods) N-COUNT
A method is a particular way of doing something.

misuse (misuses, misusing, misused) VERB [v n]
If someone misuses something, they use it incorrectly, carelessly, or dishonestly.

n

network (networks, networking, networked) VERB [BUSINESS]
If you network, you try to meet new people who might be useful to you in your job.

o

observe (observes, observing, observed) VERB [FORMAL]
If you observe a person or thing, you watch them carefully, especially in order to learn something about them.

Presenting

overcome (overcomes, overcoming, overcame) VERB
If you overcome a problem or feeling, you successful deal with it and control it.

p

pace N-SING
The pace of something is the speed at which it happens or is done.

paraphrase (paraphrases, paraphrasing, paraphrased) VERB
If you paraphrase someone or paraphrase something that they have said or written, you express what they have said or written in a different way.

plagiarize (plagiarizes, plagiarizing, plagiarized) [in BRIT, also use plagiarise] VERB
If somebody plagiarizes another person's idea or work, they use it or copy it and pretend that they thought of it or created it.

portrait N-UNCOUNT
Portrait is the way of printing a document in which the sides of the page are longer than the top and bottom.

postgraduate (postgraduates) [in AM, use graduate student] N-COUNT
A postgraduate or a postgraduate student is a student with a first degree from a university who is studying or doing research at a more advanced level.

posture (postures) N-VAR
Your posture is the position in which you stand or sit.

pressurized [in BRIT, also use pressurised] ADJ [usu ADJ N]
If you are in a pressurized situation or environment, you feel stressed and worried because what you have to do is difficult or you do not have much time to do it.

prevent (prevents, preventing, prevented) VERB
To prevent something means to ensure that it does not happen.

r

ratio (ratios) N-COUNT [usu sing]
A ratio is a relationship between two things when it is expressed in numbers or amounts. For example, if there are ten boys and thirty girls in a room, the ratio of boys to girls is 1:3, or one to three.

readability N-UNCOUNT
The readability of a document is how clear and easy it is to read.

realistic ADJ [usu v-link ADJ]
You say that a situation, painting, story, or film is realistic when the people and things in it are like people and things in real life.

recommendation (recommendations) N-VAR [oft with poss]
A recommendation of something is the suggestion that someone should have or use it because it is good.

redirect (redirects, redirecting, redirected) VERB
If you redirect your energy, resources, or ability, you begin doing something different or trying to achieve something different.

rehearsal (rehearsals) N-VAR
A rehearsal of a presentation, play, dance, or piece of music is a practice of it in preparation for a performance.

rehearse (rehearses, rehearsing, rehearsed) VERB
When people rehearse a presentation, play, dance, or piece of music, they practise it in order to prepare for a performance.

relief (reliefs) N-VAR
If you feel a sense of relief, you feel happy because something unpleasant has not happened or is no longer happening.

repeatedly ADV [ADV with v]
If you do something repeatedly, you do it many times.

representative ADJ
Someone who is typical of the group to which they belong can be described as representative.

resolve (resolves, resolving, resolved) VERB [FORMAL]
To resolve a problem, argument, or difficulty means to find a solution to it.

rush (rushes, rushing, rushed) [VERB]
If you rush, you do something too quickly because you do not have much time.

s

script (scripts) N-COUNT
A script is a text that is written in full sentences to
be read out exactly as it is written.

selective ADJ
When someone is selective, they choose things
carefully, for example the things that they buy
or do.

set ADJ [usu ADJ N]
A set book must be studied by students taking a
particular course.

setting (settings) N-COUNT
A particular setting is a particular place or type
of surroundings where something is or takes
place.

sophisticated ADJ
If something is sophisticated, it is advanced or
complex.

spontaneous ADJ
Spontaneous acts are not planned or arranged, but
are done because someone suddenly wants to do
them.

stance (stances) N-COUNT [usu sing]
Your stance on a particular matter is your opinion
on or your attitude to it.

stiff (stiffer, stiffest) ADJ
Something that is stiff is firm or does not bend
easily.

still (stiller, stillest) ADJ [ADJ after v,v -link ADJ]
If you stay still, you stay in the same position and
do not move.

stress (stresses, stressing, stressed) VERB
If you stress a word or part of a word when you
say it, you put emphasis on it so that it sounds
slightly louder.

subtle (subtler, subtlest) ADJ
Something that is subtle is not immediately obvious
or noticeable.

suffix (suffixes) N-COUNT
A suffix is a letter or group of letters, for example
'-ly' or '-ness', which is added to the end of a
word in order to form a different word, often of
a different word class. For example, the suffix
'-ly' is added to 'quick' to form 'quickly'.

sympathize (sympathizes, sympathizing,
sympathized) [in BRIT, also use sympathise] VERB
If you sympathize with someone's feelings, you
understand them and are not critical of them.

t

terminology (terminologies) N-VAR
The terminology of a subject is the set of special
words and expressions used in connection with it.

terminology (terminologies) N-VAR
The terminology of a subject is the set of special
words and expressions used in connection with it.

thorough ADJ
A thorough action or activity is done very carefully
and in a detailed way so that nothing is forgotten.

thoroughly ADV [ADV WITH V]
If you do something thoroughly, you do it very
carefully and in a detailed way so that nothing is
forgotten.

topic (topics) N-COUNT
A topic is a particular subject that you can discuss
or write about.

u

unique ADJ
Something that is unique is the only one of its kind.

unnecessary ADJ
If you describe something as unnecessary, you mean
that it is not needed or does not have to be done,
and is undesirable.

unobtrusively ADV [usu ADV with v]
If you describe something or someone as
unobtrusive, you mean that they are not easily
noticed or do not draw attention to themselves.

v

vocal cords N-PLURAL
Your vocal cords are the part of your throat that
vibrates when you speak.

Audio scripts

Chapter 2 Seminars and tutorials

Track 01

Speaker A: One thing I found interesting was that 80 per cent of the country's income goes to 20 per cent of the population.

Speaker B: Yeah. I thought that was important too, because it shows the inequality in the country.

Track 02

See the text in Exercise 5.

Track 03

So, today I'm going to talk about the effects of the internet on the newspaper industry in the USA. This is an interesting topic because the internet has really changed how we get our news, and traditional news outlets have been really affected and sometimes haven't coped very well.

Tracks 04 and 05

The biggest impact on the newspaper business model has been the difference between reading news on a daily basis versus having a continual updating stream of news available for free on the internet. By the time a newspaper arrives at your front door in the morning, you have probably already read about the earthquake in Asia or the latest political scandal in Washington DC. Furthermore, along with traditional online news outlets like newspaper websites, people are turning to alternative online sources, for example, reading political blogs rather than political coverage in the paper.

Chapter 3 Planning and structuring formal presentations

Track 06

Hello everyone – thanks for coming today. My name's Teresa Sousa and the topic I want to talk about today is the problems countries in the developing world have with exporting goods.

One thing you might not know about exports from the developing world is that developing countries obtain 32 times as much revenue from exports as they do from aid from developed nations, so exports are really crucial to these countries.

In my presentation today, I'm first going to talk about the kinds of goods exported by developing countries in Africa and Asia. Then I'm going to look at restrictions they face from the US and the EU. Finally, I'm going to talk about the positive effects that even a small increase on exports could have on developing nations.

Track 07

I'm Teresa Sousa.

My name's Teresa Sousa.

The topic I want to talk about today is problems countries in the developing world have ...

This morning, I'm going to focus on problems countries in the developing world have…

Today I'm going to outline and discuss problems countries in the developing world have…

One thing you might not know about exports from the developing world is developing countries obtain 32 times as much revenue …

Did you know that developing countries obtain 32 times as much revenue…?

Have you ever thought about why countries in the developing world are unable to export…?

I'm first going to talk about the kinds of goods exported by developing countries in Africa and Asia. Then I'm going to look at restrictions they face from the US and the EU. Finally, I'm going to talk about the positive effects that even a small increase on exports could have on developing nations.

I'm going to start by looking at the kinds of goods exported by developing countries in Africa and Asia. Then I'll move on to restrictions they face from the US and the EU. To finish, I'll talk to you about the positive effects that even a small increase on exports could have on developing nations.

My presentation is divided into three parts. First, I'm going to talk about the kinds of goods exported by developing countries in Africa and Asia. Second, I'm going to look at restrictions they face from the US and the EU. Third, I'm going to talk about the positive effects that even a small increase on exports could have on developing nations.

Track 08

1 … finally, I'll look at the positive effects that even a small increase on exports could have on developing nations. So, moving on to the kinds of goods exported by developing countries in Africa and Asia, …

2 … so you can see the kinds of products that are typically available for export. Let's turn to the kinds of the restrictions countries in the developing world have to deal with, perhaps the first thing to say is …

3 … and that's why countries in the developing world continue to have problems. Let's look now at what would happen if countries in the developing world were able to increase their exports.

4 I'd like to conclude by reviewing the three areas I looked at in this presentation.

Track 09

I'd like to conclude by reviewing the three areas I looked at in this presentation. First, we saw the different kinds of goods that developing countries in Africa and Asia typically export. Then we looked at the kinds of restrictions these countries face from the US and the EU. Finally, we saw how countries in the developing world would benefit from even a small increase in exports. I argued that the trade restrictions we looked at have a really negative effect on the poorest countries in the world. I'd like you to imagine how people's lives in these countries would be different if the restrictions didn't exist. Thank you for listening. Are there any questions?

Track 10

1 Now Sara is going to talk about …

2 Next, Mehmet will move on to …

3 Xu Li is now going to look at …

Presenting

Chapter 4 Making and using notes

Track 11

So, moving on to high-speed rail in the USA. I think perhaps the first thing to say is that 'high-speed' doesn't mean, ah, the same in the US as it does in … some other countries. Erm, in the US, the …, the top speed of high-speed lines is typically from 180 to 240 kilometres an hour, … which isn't as much as in a lot of other countries.

At the moment, high-speed rail seems to be becoming more attractive to Americans, and, er, there are different reasons for this. The most important reasons are probably high fuel prices making using the car or flying more expensive than it used to be, airport security making the experience of air travel less pleasant, and environmental concerns – so, um, people generally worrying more about how cars and planes damage the environment.

Ah, it looks like the US government's um …, taking high-speed rail quite seriously. In 2009, the government agreed to spend about *eight billion dollars* on high-speed rail. There are ten strategic corridors that they're planning to develop.

Chapter 5 Using your voice

Track 12

1 My presentation is divided into three parts.

2 First, I'll give a summary of the current situation.

3 Now let's look at the graph.

4 At the end of the presentation, I'll give you all a copy of the results.

Track 13

1 OK, let's call her.

2 OK, let's have a look at the results of the survey.

Track 14

1 OK, let's move on to the next part.

2 Right, let's turn to the situation in the early part of the year.

3 So, what can we do to solve the problem?

4 Now, let's think about what makes the policy so successful.

Track 15

There are 15 members in the UN Security Council. There are five permanent members, and they all have to agree or the Council can't make a decision.

Track 16

1 Let's look now at web browsers. I'm going to talk about three browsers – Opera, Safari and Firefox.

2 An eclipse is basically when a planet or star becomes invisible. A solar eclipse is when the moon passes between the Sun and the Earth.

3 We'll see two main kinds of language variation: geographic variation, and social variation.

Track 17

There are three areas to think about.

Track 18

1 The map shows the main towns and cities in the area.

 a /ænd/

 b The weak form of 'and' is /ənd/. When 'and' is placed between two nouns the /d/ is often silent so you will hear /ən/.

2 I want to look now at the negative consequences.

 a /aɪ/

 b /ə/

3 The policies were very effective.

 a /wə/

 b /wɜ:/

4 We can look at this again at the end.

 a /kən/

 b /kæn/

5 'Lula' da Silva was president of Brazil from 2003 to 2010.

 a /ɒv/

 b /əv/

Track 19

I'm going to talk about a number of issues and ideas.

Track 20

My presentation is divided into three parts.

Track 21

1 The media are very powerful.

2 We only want to talk about one specific aspect of this.

3 There are two other important points

Track 22

1 We asked them to complete the questionnaire within a week.

2 We can't be sure of the exact number.

3 Genghis Khan lived between 1155 and 1227.

4 The next part of my presentation will explain why.

5 I haven't got a library card.

6 This is the last day of my course.

Chapter 7 Engaging your audience

Track 23
We can't be sure why the empire fell, but we can make some good guesses.

Track 24
That's not what we're going to analyse today.

Track 25
1 We do need to think about some other factors.

2 This has happened before in other tests.

3 The antivirus software should detect it, but it doesn't.

4 This result did surprise us, as it was the opposite of what we expected.

5 It doesn't matter now, but I think it will be important in future.

Chapter 8 How to use visual aids

Track 26
1 As you can see in this table, there are four …

2 This graph shows the results of the …

3 If you look at this slide, what you can see is an increase in the number of …

4 Have a look at this graph.

5 If we move on to the next slide, we can see why …

6 I'd like you to look at this table, which shows all the different figures …

Track 27
OK, so have a look at this chart. It shows the percentage of the population staying on in education after the age of 16, in 2000 and 2010. If you just look at the left part of the chart, you can see that the number of young people staying on beyond 16 has increased in that ten-year period. But take a closer look at the centre part. You can see that the number staying on beyond 17 was the same in 2000 and 2010. Now focus on the part on the right – here we can see that the number staying on past 18 has actually fallen.

Track 28
What this shows us is that while there are fewer people leaving school at 16, there are also fewer people staying in education at 18, meaning fewer people going on to study for higher-level qualifications.

Track 29
This graph shows the GDP of the United States from 1946 to 1996 and the percentage of people who said they were 'very happy' in those years. If you just look at the left of the graph, you can see that between 1947 and 1956, GDP and happiness increased together. Now focus on the rest of the graph – since 1956, happiness has decreased, even though GDP has more than doubled. The message here is that an increase in GDP doesn't seem to make people happier.

Track 30
1 OK, so as you can see in this table … Well, sorry but the table isn't displaying properly. Let's forget that one and look at the next one.

2 Now have a look at this. Oh, the sound isn't working. Sorry about that. You can see him speaking, but … Let me just try to … No. OK, well, if the sound was working, you'd hear the speaker saying that he thinks the most important thing in the design of a mobile phone is the …

3 Now, what do you think about this? Oh, no. That's the wrong slide. Where's the other one? I definitely have it somewhere. Umm … Perhaps it's over here. Yes, I think I've found it … OK! Here we are, …

Chapter 11 Avoiding and solving problems

Track 31

Just give me a second to think about …

Just a moment, where was I …

One thing I should have said before is that some of the …

I forgot to say earlier that when we looked at …

Sorry, perhaps that wasn't very clear. The important thing is …

Let me just say that again. What you can see here is …

Sorry, no. I meant to say that not all of the …

Actually, I got that wrong. It's not the first number …

Track 32

Sorry, could you repeat that?

So I think your question is about whether or not …

Let me just think about that.

Hmm, that's an interesting question.

It might be because there were more than three different …

I suppose it's possible that they didn't know what would …

Juan, do you want to answer that one?

I think I can answer that one.

Chapter 12 Poster presentations

Track 33

My poster shows how educational programmes can have a positive effect on the fitness of high school children. The idea is that by providing education on the importance of fitness and giving advice on exercise, you can encourage high school children to improve fitness on their own. We looked at one school here in the local area and found out about the exercise habits of children before and after the programme. The results we found from this were that children exercised more after attending the programme, as you can see here. This has implications for educational policy-makers and could be important for the fight against the increasing amount of obesity in the country.

Answer key

Chapter 1

Exercise 1

1 c 2 d 3 a 4 b

Exercise 2

1 speaking in public

2 language skills

3 do not know much about the topic

4 worry about what to include

5 give presentations in groups

Exercise 3

Features to tick:

- anticipating problems

- using effective body language and eye contact

- using visual aids effectively

- engaging with your audience

- being well organized

- planning and rehearsing

- including relevant content

- speaking effectively

The three features which are *not* appropriate: giving as much detail as possible, making the audience laugh and writing a script and reading it carefully.

Exercise 4

giving as much detail as possible: You need to be careful not to include too much detail, as it will make your presentation difficult to follow. It is better for you to select your information carefully and to deliver a clear and simple message.

making the audience laugh: Your presentation might contain some humour, but this is not necessary. Remember that something considered amusing in one culture may not be acceptable in another and that academic presentations should be quite formal.

writing a script and reading it carefully: It is not a good idea to read word for word from a script, because this will sound unnatural. It will also be difficult for your audience to follow. You should use notes instead of a script and deliver your presentation by talking, rather than by reading.

Exercise 5

1 being well organized 2 including relevant content 3 speaking effectively 4 using effective body language and eye contact 5 engaging with your audience 6 using visual aids effectively 7 planning and rehearsing 8 anticipating problems

Chapter 2

Exercise 1

Answers will vary. Each student has a unique response, according to their situation.

Exercise 2

Answers will vary. Suggested answers only.

1 It is natural to worry about making mistakes, either with the language you use or the content of what you say. Remember that many other students in the seminar will have similar feelings. If you have the courage to speak in the group setting, they may be so impressed by your confidence that they will not be listening for your mistakes. You have probably had to pass a number of English exams to get into your university, so remember your success in them to give yourself confidence.

2 There are no easy solutions for this, but good preparation for the discussion should help. If you have reading to do for the seminar, read *actively* not *passively* – underline and make notes about the most important and interesting parts of the text, and try to react personally and think about *your* opinions on what you read. If the seminar follows a lecture, reread your lecture notes and

do the same thing – underline the parts you think are important or interesting, and try to react personally to the content. This way, you should have some specific ideas that you are ready to talk about when you go into the seminar.

3 Following the same advice as for 2 should help you. The most important thing is to try and prepare by reacting personally to any texts or lectures that will be discussed in the seminar. Think about what you agree or disagree with and, most importantly, *why*.

4 It is normal to be worried about how you will be assessed. However, remember that if you participate in the discussion, you will receive more credit than if you stay silent.

5 This is one of the reasons universities offer seminars. If you do not understand something, a seminar is a perfect opportunity to ask for explanation. You will learn more about how to do this in this chapter.

Exercise 3

1 It seems that most governments in the world aren't interested in stopping climate change.

2 Perhaps we need to think about parenting in a different context.

3 The policy might work better in the developed world.

4 I'd say there are a lot of reasons why the cold war ended.

5 In a sense, both writers are making the same point about modernism.

6 Maybe stable prices are impossible in the economy at the moment.

7 I think, in a way, that looking at human rights as universal isn't always right.

8 I think it's sort of old-fashioned to think of the internet like that.

Exercise 4

1 It seems that the EU's economic policies aren't working.

2 The people interviewed for the survey might not represent the whole of society.

3 Maybe there were other reasons for the conflict.

4 I'd say that in the future, the email system like it is today won't exist any more.

5 I think it wasn't a free and fair election.

Exercise 5

The change of turn happened at the end of the first speaker's sentence. We do not know if she had finished speaking so she may have been interrupted.

Exercise 6

1 c 2 a 3 b

Exercise 7

So what the writer is saying is that the rich world promises the poor world prosperity, but it doesn't happen because of all the reasons he gives at the beginning?

So does the writer mean that people in the developing world are still poor and hungry, even though the rich world continues to tell them that their situation will improve?

Exercise 8

1 d (the negative word is 'though')

2 a

3 b

4 c

Exercise 9

She introduces the topic and says why it is interesting.

Exercise 10

You probably found the text difficult to follow. It contains a lot of information and it is hard to understand the important points.

Exercise 11

This time, you probably found it easier to listen to. The speaker made more pauses and also stressed the important parts more clearly, to emphasize them.

Presenting

Exercise 12

What can an <u>industry do</u> | when all of its
value | is in the process of being replaced by a
resource that is <u>almost free</u> | to the <u>consumer</u>?
Most newspapers | have <u>responded</u> | by <u>adapting</u>
to the new reality, | offering as <u>much up-to-
date news</u> on their <u>websites</u>, | <u>changing</u> their
<u>business model</u> | to rely <u>increasingly</u> on <u>internet</u>
advertising revenue | instead of <u>sales</u> and
<u>print</u> advertising. | <u>Some papers</u> | have gone
<u>further,</u> | deciding to <u>adapt</u> | to the more <u>interactive
nature</u> | of the <u>internet</u> | and <u>allowing readers</u> to
<u>participate</u> | by <u>commenting</u> on <u>articles</u> | or even
<u>writing new ones</u>. | But for <u>some newspapers</u>, | <u>this
strategy</u> | has <u>not</u> been totally <u>successful</u>.

Chapter 3

Exercise 1
Answers will vary. Suggested answers only.

You could focus just on financial problems faced
by higher education institutions, like universities.
Alternatively, you could look at the needs of
employers and how the skills they need are often
different from what students learn at school.

Exercise 2
a 4

b 2

c 3

d 5

e 7

f 1

g 6

Exercise 3
Answers will vary. Suggested answers only.

Basic organization:

three types of school: primary school, middle
school, high school

age you go to school and university

types of university

Educational philosophy:

focus on learning facts

frequent examinations

focus on basic skills like reading, writing and
mathematics

Strengths and weaknesses:

does not provide much preparation for the
workplace

school leavers have good writing and mathematics
skills

does not develop analytical skills

Exercise 4
Answers will vary.

Exercise 5
a 5

b 2

c 4

d 1

e 3

Exercise 6
Introducing yourself

I'm **Teresa Sousa**.
My name's **Teresa Sousa**.

Introducing the topic

The topic **I want to talk about** today is problems
countries in the developing world have …

This morning I'm going to **focus on** problems
countries in the developing world have …

Today I'm going to **outline** and **discuss** problems
countries in the developing world have …

Getting the audience interested

One thing **you might not know** about exports from
the developing world is developing countries obtain
32 times as much revenue …

Did you **know that** developing countries obtain
32 times as much revenue …?

Have you ever **thought about** why countries in the
developing world are unable to export … ?

Giving the structure of your presentation

I'm **first** going to talk about the kinds of good exported by developing countries in Africa and Asia./ **Then** I'm going to look at restrictions they face from the US and the EU./ **Finally**, I'm going to talk about the positive effects that even a small increase on exports could have on developing nations.

I'm going to **start by** looking at the kinds of good exported by developing countries in Africa and Asia. / Then I'll **move on** to restrictions they face from the US and the EU. / **To finish**, I'll talk to you about the positive effects that even a small increase on exports could have on developing nations.

My presentation **is divided into** three parts. First, I'm going to talk about the kinds of goods exported by developing countries in Africa and Asia. / Second, I'm going to look at restrictions they face from the US and the EU. / Third, I'm going to talk about the positive effects that even a small increase on exports could have on developing nations.

Exercise 7

So, moving on to …

Let's turn to …

Let's look now at …

I'd like to conclude by …

Exercise 8

The phrases to use only in a spoken presentation are:

X says that …

Here you can see X's definition of …

The other three phrases are suitable for both presentation and essay use.

Exercise 9

a 2

b 4

c *5*

d *1*

e 3

Exercise 10

1 c   2 d   3 a   4 b

Exercise 11

1 b   2 c   3 a

Exercise 12

Now Sara is going to talk about …

Next, Mehmet will move on to …

Xu Li is now going to look at …

Chapter 4

Exercise 1

1 nouns and verbs are used with equal frequency: S
In spoken language, we use about as many nouns as we do verbs. In written, academic language, however, we typically use three or four times as many nouns as verbs.

2 long noun phrases are used frequently: W
Long noun phrases appear more frequently in written than spoken language. Compare these two sentences:

- The questionnaire, *which was sent out in May and completed by over 10,000 respondents from all over the country*, revealed some interesting trends.

- We created a questionnaire and sent it out in May. It was completed by over 10,000 people from all over the country and it revealed some interesting trends.

3 first and second personal pronouns *(I, me, we, us, you)* are much more common: S
In academic writing, first and second person pronouns are uncommon. In spoken language, however, they are commonplace.

4 grammar words (e.g. auxiliary verbs, prepositions, articles) are used more frequently: S

5 the range of vocabulary is smaller: S

Written texts usually use a much wider range of vocabulary. When you read something alone, you have the chance to look up the words you do not know in a dictionary. The audience, listening to a presentation, cannot do this.

Exercise 2
Answers will vary.

Exercise 3
Answers will vary.

Exercise 4
Answers will vary. Suggested answer.

> _International Space Station_
> _orbit: 240 statue miles_
> _17,500 km/h_
> _cooperation between 5 space agencies / 16 countries_
>
> _November 2000: first crew – max. 6 when fully crewed_
> _station = laboratory, experiments in many areas_
> _inc. future technologies, base for missions to Moon, Mars,_
> _asteroids_
> _gravity similar to Earth – weightlessness from falling_

Exercise 5
Answers will vary.

Exercise 6
The presenter has made notes to: remind himself or herself to not talk too quickly, to make eye contact with the audience and to change the slide on the visual aid.

Chapter 5

Exercise 1
Answers will vary.

Exercise 2
Answers will vary.

Exercise 3
The ideal time taken in reading the text would be about 45 seconds. If you took about 30 seconds, you should slow down a little, paying attention to pausing to emphasize the key points. If it took you closer to 60 seconds, you were going too slowly. Try it again and increase your pace.

Exercise 4
1 ↘   2 ↗

3 ↘   4 ↗

Exercise 5
In sentence 1, 'OK' is spoken with normal falling intonation. In sentence 2, it is spoken with a rise-fall intonation.

Exercise 6
No answer required.

Exercise 7
1 _revenue_: three syllables; _developing_: four syllables. The syllables are shown with a vertical line: |;

2 The first syllable is stressed in _revenue_. The second syllable is stressed in _developing_. This is shown in the dictionary by the fact that the stressed syllable is underlined in the phonemic transcription: /ˈrevɪnjuː/, /dɪˈveləpɪŋ/.

Exercise 8
The words 'member' and 'Council' are not stressed, because they do not contain _new_ information. The speaker has already mentioned the council and the members in the previous sentence. In the second sentence, as they are less important, they are not stressed.

Exercise 9
1 Let's look now at web browsers. I'm going to talk about three browsers – Opera, Safari and Firefox.

2 An eclipse is basically when a planet or star becomes invisible. A solar eclipse is when the moon passes between the Sun and the Earth.

3 We'll see two main kinds of language variation: geographic variation, and social variation.

Exercise 10

The words *are* and *to* are said very fast, with a short, neutral vowel sound. This sound is called a 'schwa'. To make the 'schwa' sound /ə/, you need to relax your mouth and tongue completely. It is often difficult to hear a 'schwa' because they are pronounced quickly and at a lower volume.

Exercise 11

1 b   2 b   3 a   4 a   5 b

Exercise 12

1 b

2 c

3 a

Exercise 13

1 The sounds /k/ and /t/ are not pronounced in 'asked' and 'them'.

2 The sound /t/ is not pronounced in 'can't'.

3 The sound /d/ is not pronounced in 'lived'.

4 The sound /t/ is not pronounced in 'next'.

5 The sound /t/ is not pronounced in 'haven't'.

6 The sound /t/ is not pronounced in 'last'.

Chapter 6

Exercise 1

You would probably feel very calm. You would walk in a relaxed way, probably quite slowly.

Exercise 2

1 In a small room, you would probably sit.

2 If you are using visual aids, you would probably stand.

3 This would depend very much on the context – the number of people, the size of the room, what other students do.

If you are in doubt, ask your lecturer whether you are expected to sit or stand while presenting.

Exercise 3

1
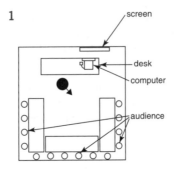

2
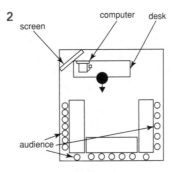

3
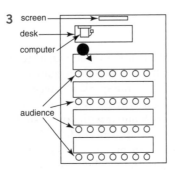

4
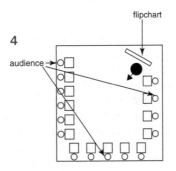

Presenting

1 The best position is in front of the desk, in the centre. The speaker might find it difficult to access the computer, but could ask somebody to help. Alternatively, the mouse appears to be easy to reach, so it may be possible to use the computer without help.

2 The best position is in front of the desk, in the centre. The presenter needs to make sure not to block the audience's view of the screen, however, especially the people to the right.

3 As the screen is in the centre, it is better for the presenter to stand away from the centre, although if the screen is high enough this might not be necessary. The best position is near the computer, if the computer is needed. It would also be possible for the presenter to stand on the other side, if the computer was not needed or if there was somebody to help the presenter.

4 The best position is near the flipchart. If the presenter stands more towards the centre, the audience at the front left will probably not be able to see the flipchart. The presenter needs to be careful not to block the view of the audience sitting nearby.

Exercise 4

1 The presenter is looking at the visual aid, instead of at the audience. This means that the audience might not be able to hear the speaker's voice well and the audience may feel less involved. It is advisable to be very familiar with your visual aids, so you can talk about them confidently and without looking at them much. It is fine to look at them from time to time, but make sure you turn back towards the audience as often as possible.

2 In this illustration, the speaker is blocking the screen, so the audience probably cannot see any of the visual aids presented. The speaker might need to block the screen occasionally (e.g. to point at something), but should move out of the way again as soon as possible. Alternatively, you can use a pointing stick or a laser pen to point at things without getting in the way of the screen. If you are using PowerPoint, you can set up slides to highlight certain points. For more information on PowerPoint, see Chapter 9.

3 In this illustration, the speaker is standing behind the computer, which may block the audience's view. It is not advisable to have obstructions between the speaker and the audience. If the speaker must go to the computer to change a slide, then the speaker should move back to the home position as soon as possible. The speaker could get somebody to help manage the computer for them.

4 The speaker is very far away from the computer so he or she will have to walk across the room to show the slide, which could be a distraction. It is a good idea to stay close to any visual aid equipment you need to use, or alternatively to ask someone to help you. In this case, another person could sit by the computer and show the slide when the presenter is ready.

Exercise 5

Answers will vary.

Exercise 6

1 g

2 e

3 c

4 f

5 d

6 b

7 a

8 i

9 h

Exercise 7

a 1

b 5

c 4

d 2

e 8

f 3

g 7

h 9

i 6

Chapter 7

Exercise 1

1 j

2 d

3 a

4 e

5 c

6 h

7 f

8 b

9 i

10 g

Exercise 2

1 b

2 a

3 a

Exercise 3

1 main 2 go back 3 work out 4 quite
5 happen 6 a lot of 7 look at 8 show

Exercise 4

1 c

2 a

3 b

Exercise 5

1 c

2 b

3 d

4 a

5 f

6 e

Exercise 8

1 do 2 has 3 should 4 did 5 will

Exercise 9

1 What I want to talk about today is <u>tardigrades, which are tiny animals also known as 'water bears'</u>.

2 What you need to do is <u>to write what you think the answer is in the box</u>.

3 What we need to think about is <u>where the waste will be stored</u>.

4 What we should remember is <u>that the participants in the study might not be representative</u>.

Exercise 10

1 (What) you're going to see now is a summary of the results. (emphasizing the object)

2 (What) we should think about is how to improve the research methods. (emphasizing the *Wh-* clause)

3 (What) they thought was that the website design would increase profits. (emphasizing the *that* clause)

4 (What) I'd like you to do is (to) keep this image in your head while I speak. (emphasizing the verb)

5 (What) we looked at then was where the biggest technological innovations seem to be happening. (emphasizing the *Wh-* clause)

6 (What) we need to do is (to) look at some of these results in more depth. (emphasizing the verb)

7 (What) I showed you earlier was a photo of the nuclear reactor. (emphasizing the object)

8 (What) we hope is that we'll have some more definite results next year. (emphasizing the *that* clause)

Exercise 11

1 There are a lot of important consequences of genetically modified foods, but I think it's the impact on the environment that's the most significant.

2 It's investment that the country needs, not loans.

3 The phrase 'united nations' was first used officially in 1942, but it was in 1945 that the organization was created.

4 The United Nations has offices in Geneva, Nairobi and Vienna, but it's in New York that the General Assembly is held.

Exercise 12
1 f

2 a

3 e

4 b

5 c

6 d

Chapter 8

Exercise 1
Since there is a limit to how much information people can take in with their eyes or ears, it is better to get the audience to use both when you give a presentation. Visual aids help with learning, because the audience can process more information if the presenter speaks (giving verbal information) and uses visual aids (visual information) at the same time.

Exercise 2
1 overhead projector   2 handout
3 PowerPoint presentation (or video)
4 flipchart   5 whiteboard
6 interactive whiteboard

Exercise 3
1 whiteboards/blackboards   2 PowerPoint presentations, possibly video recordings   3 handouts, PowerPoint presentations   4 handouts   5 flip charts
6 all apart from blackboards/whiteboards

Exercise 4
1 Probably a handout and/or the whiteboard. For a short presentation like this, you would probably not be expected to prepare a PowerPoint presentation.

2 Since you have not finished the research, you probably will not be expected to prepare a very sophisticated presentation. You could use any of the visual aids discussed.

3 You will not have time to prepare anything, but you could use a whiteboard to support your points.

4 You will need some well-prepared visual aids. You should at least prepare information on a flipchart, if it is available. Most people would probably prepare OHPs or a PowerPoint presentation, perhaps with some handouts.

Exercise 5
1 True – spoken words are easier to follow than written words.

2 False – images help the audience to follow the presentation.

3 True – irrelevant information makes it harder for the audience to follow a presentation.

4 False – you should explain ideas verbally; text in a visual aid should be limited and should at most confirm what you have said, not add to it.

Exercise 6
1 There is too much text. It would be better to reduce the text to just the key words.

2 There is too much irrelevant text. The student's name and the course name would have already appeared on the first slide, so they should not appear here. Likewise, the information about the university (the university logo, the illustration on the right) should also be removed.

3 Images would be helpful in this context, instead of or together with the text.

4 The image here is irrelevant and inappropriate for a presentation. It should be removed.

Exercise 7
Answers will vary. Suggested answers only.

1 1970s–present: high oil prices = recessions

2 User-centred design: end-users – every stage

3 Top-level managers: plans, goals, decisions

Exercise 8

1 As you can **see** in this table, …

2 **This** graph **shows** …

3 If you **look at** this slide, what **you** can **see** is …

4 **Have** a **look at** this graph.

5 If we **move onto** the next slide…

6 I'd **like** you to **look at** this table, which **shows**…

Exercise 9

1 come   2 see   3 explain   4 show
5 Remember   6 come

Exercise 12

1 The message here is that …   2 Looking at this, we can say that …   3 This is important, because …   4 What this highlights is that …

Exercise 13

Answers will vary.

Exercise 14

1 OHP slides   2 all visual aids apart from handouts   3 PowerPoint slides or a video (if being shown through a computer); OHP slides or a PowerPoint presentation   5 OHP slides, PowerPoint or video (they are shown by means of a computer) – remember though that if the lights are low it can be harder to read a handout or take notes; PowerPoint (this would also work for OHP slides).

Exercise 15

1 PowerPoint slide; 2 video; 3 OHP slide

2 Speaker 2 deals with the situation well. She acts quickly and just uses her own words to summarize the information that the visual aid was supposed to give.

Speaker 1 acts quickly but just skips the visual aid altogether. It is better to try and summarize like Speaker 2.

Speaker 3 spends too long trying to solve the problem. It is best to try and act quickly like Speaker 2 or your audience may become bored and frustrated.

Chapter 9

Exercise 1

Answers will vary.

Exercise 2

1 c

2 a

3 b

4 e

5 f

6 h

7 d

8 g

Exercise 3

1 lots of text   2 in order of importance
3 complex information   4 what you are saying

Exercise 4

1 c

2 d

3 b

4 a

Exercise 5

1 No

2 No

3 Yes

4 Yes

5 No

6 Yes

Exercise 6

1 a

2 b

3 a

4 b

Exercise 7

1 small 2 smaller 3 Sans serif
4 two or three 5 simple 6 one transition effect

Chapter 10

Exercise 1

This behaviour will make a poor impression on the lecturer. The lecturer will want to have a realistic presentation atmosphere in the room, with the audience paying attention and listening carefully to each presentation.

The other presenters or students will be disturbed by this behaviour taking place while they are speaking. Seeing the audience talking or working on their laptops can be distracting and annoying for the presenter. If you pay no attention when others are presenting, you may find that when it is your turn to speak, others will do the same to you.

Exercise 2

1 automatic 2 timing 3 technology
4 whole 5 problems 6 voice

Exercise 3

1 d

2 b

3 a

4 e

5 c

Exercise 4

1 position 2 space 3 lighting 4 access
5 layout

Exercise 5

1 c

2 b

3 a

4 c

5 a

6 b

Exercise 6

Suggested answers appear in the chapter.

Exercise 7

1 b

2 e

3 f

4 c

5 d

6 a

Exercise 8

Answers will vary.

Exercise 9

Answers will vary.

Exercise 10

Answers will vary.

Chapter 11

Exercise 1

1 b

2 c

3 a

4 d

Exercise 2

1 Do

2 Do

3 Don't

4 Do

5 Don't

Exercise 3

Giving yourself time when your mind goes blank

Just give me <u>a second</u> …

Just a <u>moment</u> …

Saying something you forgot to say earlier

One thing I should have said before is …

I forgot to say earlier that …

Rephrasing something that you didn't say clearly

Sorry, perhaps that wasn't very clear.

Let me just explain that again.

Correcting a factual error

Sorry, no. I meant to say …

Actually, I got that wrong …

Exercise 4

1 Predict

2 Ask

3 Give

4 worry

5 Try

Exercise 5

Asking for repetition and clarification

Sorry, could you repeat that?

So I think your question is …

Giving yourself time to think

Let me just think about that.

Hmm, that's an interesting question.

Speculating when you don't know

It might be because …

I suppose it's possible that …

Managing questions in a group presentation

Juan, do you want to answer that one?

I think I can answer that one.

Chapter 12

Exercise 1

1 d

2 a

3 c

4 b

Exercise 2

| 1 c | 2 b | 3 d | 4 a |

Exercise 3

| 1 Do | 2 Don't | 3 Don't | 4 Do |
| 5 Do | 6 Do | | |

Exercise 4

| 1 a | 2 b | 3 b | 4 b | 5 a |
| 6 a | 7 a | 8 b | | |

Exercise 5

1 appropriate

2 difficult

3 two

4 serif

5 sans serif

6 two or three

Exercise 6

1 My poster shows

2 The idea is

3 We looked at

4 The results we found from this were

5 This has implications for

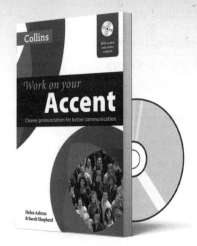